# LIVERPOOL'S CHILDREN
## in the 1950s

### PAMELA RUSSELL

The History Press

This book is for my husband, David; my son, Christopher; and my daughter-in-law, Sarah. Also for my sister and brother-in-law, Janet and Graeme Arnot; my brother-in-law, Harold Russell; my cousin, Brenda Bryce; Graeme's brother, Terry Arnot; and Sarah's parents, Ron and Shirley Evans, all of whom are Liverpool's Children

*Lord Street, Liverpool, in 1953.*

First published 2012

The History Press
The Mill, Brimscombe Port
Stroud, Gloucestershire, GL5 2QG
www.thehistorypress.co.uk

British Library Cataloguing in Publication Data.
A catalogue record for this book is available from the British Library.

ISBN 978 0 7524 5901 1

Typesetting and origination by The History Press
Printed in Great Britain

# LIVERPOOL'S
# CHILDREN
## in the 1950s

# CONTENTS

# ACKNOWLEDGEMENTS

My thanks to all the people who contacted me with stories of a 1950s' childhood or lent photographs: Mary Allport; Graeme Arnot; Janet Arnot; Terry Arnot; Philip Baker; Christine Barrett; Pauline Bennett; Bobbie Binks; Carla Bird; Robin Bird; Chris Brocklehurst; June Buckley; Harry Byatt; Michael Chapman; Ann Cowley; Peter John (Dougie) Cox; Gordon Crompton; Jean Cross; Janet Dalton; Barry Davies; Christine Deed; Barbara Doran; Betty Duncan; Cliff Duncan ; Margaret Dunford; William (Bill) Duvall; Elizabeth (Liz) Egerton; Eileen Ellis; William (Bill) Ellis; Shirley Evans; Derek Finney; Maimie Finney; Bill Fitzgerald; Pam Fitzgerald; Mike Formby; Patricia Gilbert; Joan Gillett; Margaret Gillson; Jim Greer; Charles Griffiths; Maddy Guest; John Halley; Bert Hamblet; John Hayes; Barry Hignett; Derek Jeffery; Patricia Johnson; Enid Johnston; Agnes Jones; Anne (Annie) Jones; Susan (Sue) Jones; Moira Kennedy; Eileen Kermode; William (Bill) Kermode; Linda Leaworthy; Maurice Levene; Ken Lloyd; Anne McCormick; Christine McGarry; Peter McGuiness; John McIlroy; Michael Moran; Doris Mousdale; Jean Mullen; Joan Munro; Angela Nelson; Shelagh Nugent; Tony O'Hara; Anne Orme; Mary Parkin; Arthur Parr; Janice Pickthall; Pat Plunkett; Hayley Prentice; Eileen Pritchard; Pamela Rattray; Joan Riding; Hazel Rimmer; Madeleine Roberts; Margaret Roberts; Sylvia Roberts; David Russell; Harold Russell; Alan Scott; Grahame Settle; Gillian Shaw; Patricia Shaw; Hazel Skarratts; Doreen Stock; William Stock; Joseph Swindells; Barbara Walsh; Norma White, *née* Schafer; Norma White; Lilian Williams; Patricia Williams; Susan Williams. Also Gloria Nall (*Champion Newspaper*).

For photographs and other material my thanks go to the following people: David Russell, without whose technical and photographic expertise none of these photographs would have appeared; Christopher Russell for the Liver Bird; Robin Bird for permission to use photographs from the Bob Bird Collection and Val Stephens for the loan of her father's comprehensive diaries.

# ABOUT THE AUTHOR

Pamela Russell (M.Phil) is a retired Senior Lecturer of Edge Hill University, Ormskirk, Lancashire.

# INTRODUCTION

This is the story of the children of Liverpool, and the surrounding area, growing up in the 1950s. It includes as many people's memories as possible – told in their own words – and aims to capture the warmth and excitement of their childhood and teenage years, set against the wider background of the events of the period. The fifties is a decade that is often dismissed as being dominated by the struggle to recover from the Second World War; in material terms it is depicted as a period when there was still rationing and austerity, and in social terms it is seen as a period of repression and greyness.

In fact, the fifties was a decade that saw huge change and progress, and an explosion of colour and exciting ideas. At the beginning, despite some hardships, it was a time when people were just happy to be at peace, to know that when they came home from work or shopping, their house would still be standing. They took pleasure in unsophisticated pastimes; it was a time when the company of friends and family was a matter for rejoicing. People felt relieved that anxiety was no longer their constant companion. There may have been some good-natured grumbling, but it was philosophical in tone – 'Mustn't grumble!' was a frequent comment.

As the decade progressed, life opened out. There was a new feeling that perseverance in hardship was finally being rewarded. Rationing was gradually disappearing and, when sweet rationing ended on 5 February 1953, everyone, especially children, rejoiced. Suddenly, on the shelves were old favourites and new delights to discover; children entered a wonderland of dolly mixtures, sherbet fountains, Chocstix, gobstoppers, midget gems, cherry lips, aniseed balls, liquorice torpedoes, alphabet letters, chewing nuts and Rowntree's fruit gums.

There were new and exciting inventions available to most people – television is the most obvious, with programmes like *Bill & Ben the Flowerpot Men* and *Rag, Tag and Bobtail* for younger children; *The Adventures of Robin Hood*, *The Buccaneers* and *Ivanhoe* for older children and, for the newly recognised 'teenagers', all the excitement of rock 'n' roll with *Six-Five Special* and *Juke Box Jury*. The affordability of record players and 45rpm records also changed people's leisure time.

Brighter fashions in home decoration and more materialistic ambitions changed home life. A pervading optimism in adults affected the lives of children. At the beginning of the decade, when the warmth and cosiness of the family hearth, as depicted in Ovaltine advertisements, was the general ideal, a 'latchkey kid' was often seen as an object of pity. Mothers tended to stay at home, unless there was an economic necessity for them to have a job.

The post-war shortage of housing meant that many children lived in the same house as their grandparents or other family members. Families also tended to live in the same district, or even the same street, as each other, so any extra childcare that was needed often stayed within the family. In the later fifties, labour-saving devices meant that many women could fit in, at least part-time, work outside the home and men began to welcome their contribution to the family budget.

The personal stories that appear in this book are the result of the generous response to my appeal for the memories of people who were children from the end of the war through to 1959. People see their 1950s' childhood and youth as a Golden Age, when freedom from constant adult supervision was accompanied by an underlying and reassuring sense of security. There is a real desire to revisit this period, and to share it with others who remember those days, and also to convince those who are younger that these were good times.

'Liverpool's Children' have been taken to include children growing up in the area stretching as far as Southport and Ormskirk, and including the Wirral. It is, perhaps, better defined as Greater Liverpool. Liverpool's traditional sense of community, strengthened by the war years, provided a secure background from which children and teenagers could welcome a second Elizabethan era.

The city was just beginning its emergence in music and sport, which was to explode into the excitement of Liverpool in the 1960s. But, already, it was possible to sense the excitement in the air!

Pamela Russell, 2012

# 1

# LIFE AT HOME

Mary Parkin, *née* Fox, lived in a house that had been built during the time of Liverpool's Edwardian splendour but had suffered the ravages of time and the Blitz:

I grew up, an only child, in Roscommon Street, Everton, in a house with a private landlord, which probably accounted for the state it was in by the 1950s. It had originally been a beautiful Edwardian terraced house with two huge cellars and two attics, as well as two large bedrooms on the second floor. At some point, probably in the war, the house had lost those houses to which it had been attached. We were on the end of a row without the luxury of a gable end, and the result was that the house was extremely damp and you could see evidence of this on the wallpaper inside the house. We had gas mantles until the landlord saw fit to install electricity, about 1952.

There were several steps which led up to the front door and I used to love washing and sand-stoning those steps, from being quite a young child.

My mum, Mary, and dad, Len, and I shared the house with my mum's parents, Liz and Bob Leatherbarrow. We had a fireplace in the parlour where I lived with my mum and dad and there was a black-leaded range with ovens on either side of the fire in the kitchen where my nana and granddad lived. Nana often black-leaded the grate and polished the brass fender and there was a black kettle that sat on the range. My granddad worked at the Tate & Lyle sugar factory.

The coalman used to deliver sacks of coal each week and throw them down into the cellar through the manhole cover at the bottom of the steps which led to the front door. I was given the task of counting them to make sure that we weren't being diddled.

I slept in my parents' bedroom in a bed in the corner. We had a fireplace in this room and they lit it occasionally, when it was really cold. When I was eleven I was moved into one of the attic bedrooms, which was freezing in the winter. I would scrape the frost off the inside of my bedroom window every morning in the winter months.

Shelagh Nugent, *née* Anderson, born in 1945, lived off Breck Road. Shelagh recalls:

We lived with my nan, in a house rented from Mr Murphy. It was damp and horrible and Mr Murphy knew about it each time he came to collect the rent and my nan 'gave him what for'! He wore a bowler hat and always had a pocketful of change for the children in the street, but his generosity did not extend to running repairs.

There were three bedrooms but the small back bedroom was uninhabitable because of the damp. We used it to store junk – old toys, old clothes, shoes, gas-masks, comics, broken furniture and anything else that might come in useful one day. Nothing was ever thrown out in those days.

My mum and dad slept in the big front bedroom. It was freezing cold and the damp patches on the ceiling were like brown cloud pictures.

I shared the middle bedroom with my nan. We had feather mattresses and they were the warmest, softest things I ever slept on. It was best when the bedding was changed and the feathers plumped up to the dimensions of a fluffy cloud. I'd leap right into the middle without disturbing the side and it was the cosiest nest anyone could wish for!

If it was very cold – ice-inside-the-window cold – I'd snuggle in with my nan, who smelled of camphorated oil, which was supposed to be good for her chain-smoking chest. She wheezed and coughed all night but it never kept me awake.

Downstairs we had a sitting room; we called it a sitting room because, as a family, we had delusions of grandeur. Everyone else had a parlour. It wasn't often used, except for my hated piano practice, but it had a three piece suite and fabulous glass-fronted cupboards on either side of the chimney breast. These were full of treasures beyond a little girl's wildest imaginings: gloriously illustrated cups and saucers with A Present from Blackpool on them; elaborate fancy plates, which were presents from Southport, Rhyl, Colwyn Bay, etc.; china crinoline ladies; pottery dogs, posh glasses that were never used.

The main living room was known as the kitchen and had a big black range. Those ranges were wonderful but most people had them ripped out as soon as they could afford to and had 'contemporary' fireplaces installed. These were ghastly tiled things in beige or grey and the hearth tiles were soon chipped, adding to their general ugliness.

In the back kitchen was a gas cooker, a meat safe on a marble slab and a kitchen cabinet with a pull-down flap. Behind the kitchen door was the dreaded coal cellar. You had to go down there with a candle to put a shilling in the gas meter and it was really spooky. I can remember the time before we had electricity and relied on gas mantles, which had to be lit with a match and went 'pop'.

William (Bill) Duvall was born in June 1950 in the Edge Hill area:

It was very hard, as it was for most people then, but the good times always out-weighed the bad. Our family was a very fragmented family; we are a mix of step-brothers and sisters and half-brothers and sisters, but, to us, we are all one family. It was my granddad's house; he lived in the front room. With ten kids it was very tight.

The wartime Blitz on Liverpool had caused a housing shortage which meant that many more children than today, like Mary, Shelagh and Bill, lived with relatives. Although aware of the benefits and closeness of that experience, they also knew that their houses were damp and that their parents and grandparents were not always happy with their treatment by private landlords. Many houses, even those that had not been hit, had been damaged by bomb blast or other damage, but people had no choice but to live in them.

Ken Lloyd was another child who lived in a large family group:

I was born in 1944 and lived in Pitville Road, Mossley Hill. It was located at the end of a row of about twenty terraced houses. Upstairs, it had four rooms: two bedrooms – one small, one large – at the front, and at the rear a combined WC and bathroom and medium-sized bedroom. Downstairs there was the hall, the sitting room at the front and the dining room and kitchen at the rear. There was a small front garden and a medium-sized back garden with a coal shed and a garden shed. At the rear of the back garden, there was a passage wide enough for car access for all the houses. Beyond this passageway, there were allotments which bordered the railway lines at Mossley Hill station.

Initially, there were eight people living in the house: grandfather, called Pop Pop, grandmother, called Nanny, Uncle Eric and Auntie Doreen, my father, mother, sister and myself. Grandfather and grandmother slept in the large bedroom, uncle and his wife in the small bedroom, and father, mother, sister and me in the medium-sized bedroom. My uncle and his wife stayed for a short time and then went to live in lodgings in Port Sunlight, and then bought a newly built house in Hunts Cross. My sister then slept in the small bedroom.

My father was a driver for the Liverpool Corporation Passenger Transport (LCPT) and drove the No. 79 bus; its route was from the Pier Head to Belle Vale, but he transferred a few years later to

*Ken Lloyd, far right in the line-up for the race, enjoys a day out with Liverpool Corporation Passenger Transport. Many companies provided outings and parties for the children of their employees.*

the No. 61 bus, from Aigburth to Seaforth. Mother was a housewife, but in 1956 went to work as a machinist, putting collars on shirts for a company called Menora, whose premises were in Sandown Lane off Wavertree Road. The shirts were mostly made for Littlewoods.

In 1957, Ken's family moved to a flat in one of five blocks of three storeys in Forthlin Road, Allerton. Forthlin Road was also the home of the McCartney family:

The group of friends I played with did not include Paul McCartney or his brother, Mike, as my friends came from the flats and not from the houses which were located in the first half of the road. Also Paul was two years older than me, but although Mike McCartney was the same age as me within one day, our paths never met as friends. I was always out playing football or riding my bike to local places, such as Calderstones Park. Maybe Paul and Mike were at home concentrating on their music. I remember girls sitting on Paul's front garden fence waiting to see him.

The Police Horse Show was held each year. It showed police horses jumping over fences or how they were used to control crowds and, similarly, how the police dogs and their handlers go about their police duties. As the back of the flats overlooked the grounds of the police cadet college, I would watch from my bedroom window. Paul writes in the National Trust Book '20 Forthlin Road' that he sat on the garden shed in his back garden to watch the Police Show.

As more housing was provided by Liverpool Corporation after the Second World War, many families moved house and took their new experiences in their stride. For many children, although the actual distance was only a few miles, the move was a change from living in town to being surrounded by the countryside.

Peter (Dougie) Cox was one of the children whose life was changed for the better by the new housing made available. Dougie recalls:

I was born on 21 March 1940 in Mill Road Hospital. My family was living in Kilin Street, off Byrom Street. My mother's family had lived there since 1910. Due to the bombing, we moved to a flat in Salisbury Road. As a child, I suffered with asthma and bronchitis and spent time in the Children's Hospital in Myrtle Street. Later, I went to a convalescent home at Pensarn, near Abergele, in North Wales.

*New housing estates meant that many Liverpool children moved to a new home.*

The Hillside estate in Huyton had been built by Liverpool Corporation in 1938, but was taken by the Government before anyone could move in. It was used for some time as a camp for enemy aliens. In 1946, we moved into a three-bedroomed house in Layford Close. It was No. 2 in a close of twenty-five houses numbered 1-26, with no No. 13!

After moving to Huyton, my health improved. Being in virtual countryside, the fresh air helped. At the back of our close was Knowsley Lane with farms and woods and fishing ponds and streams and, best of all, Lord Derby's estate – Knowsley.

As we grew up, the more adventurous of us kids would climb into the estate. This was called 'going over the wall' and some of the older lads became top poachers. The Park contained horses, cows, sheep and deer and was patrolled by mounted policemen. I think we had more freedom in those days – there was less traffic on the roads and, as kids, we were able to go pea-picking and potato-picking for a few bob, and we grew vegetables in our own back garden.

Joseph (Joe) Swindells, born in April 1945, had a twin sister, Anne. They lived in Norwood Grove, off West Derby Road, until they were eighteen months old, when the family was allocated a bungalow in Knowsley. Later, Joe had two brothers, Peter and Tom:

These bungalows were built for workers at the Royal Ordnance Factory (ROF) in Fazakerley, where both my parents worked. The bungalows were very basic but had three bedrooms, separate bathroom and toilet, living room and small kitchen. There was no wallpaper on the walls and the floor was covered with a stiff brown lino, which cracked very easily.

There was a coal fire in the living room, which was used to burn everything, including potato peelings. We had to put a shovel with newspaper across it to draw the fire. Often, this would catch fire and disappear up the chimney. The windows had metal frames that rusted with the dampness. But it was nice and cosy on winter evenings, sitting in front of a roaring fire, watching the sparks dancing in the grate.

*From left to right: Anne, Joe and Peter Swindells, outside their ROF bungalow in Knowsley.*

Michael Moran's earliest memories concern the newly built housing that appeared at this time:

One of my first memories was seeing our new house in Alderfield Drive on the Speke estate and having to walk on duck-boards to reach it because the roads were not finished. I was about three-and-a-half at the time, but it seems like yesterday. It was a three-bedroomed house and our family had ten members, consisting of Mum and Dad, three lads and five sisters, so the sleeping arrangements were that my eldest sister had the small bedroom to herself, the three youngest slept on bunks in Mum and Dad's room and me and my two brothers had one of my sisters sleeping in our room on a camp bed.

Until the Liverpool Corporation could build sufficient new permanent housing, there were alternatives. One result of the 1944 Temporary Housing Programme was the widespread introduction of prefabricated homes (prefabs), which were intended to provide an acceptable, even attractive, solution to the massive lack of housing caused by the war.

Many families were living in rented rooms with shared facilities, or with other family members. Most children, like Bill Duvall, enjoyed the company and family atmosphere and, in any case, they knew no other way of life. But, for adults, overcrowding and a lack of privacy could cause problems. Also, prefabs offered a proper home; many married women continued to work after the war ended because they were saving for a home of their own, and because they were not needed to keep house, because their mothers, or mothers-in-law, were already doing that job. It was hoped that prefabs would attract women out of the workplace and enable men, returning from war service, to take their jobs. Designed by the Ministry of Works, prefabs had proper fitted kitchens with a fridge and cooker, a toilet and bathrooms with running hot water. There was built-in storage, electric lighting and sockets. Many houses in both town and countryside lacked some, or all, of these facilities.

Liz Egerton remembers prefabs in Litherland:

I was born in January 1955 in Anderson Road, Litherland. The estate consisted of 'double-decker prefabs' which had been built just after the war as temporary accommodation. They were supposed to last about twenty years ... my mum lived in hers until she died two years ago!

June Buckley was born on 4 June 1950 in a prefab in Aster Road, Dovecot. She recalls:

We moved to Princess Drive, West Derby where I lived from the age of one until I married in 1973. I was one of ten children, with four older siblings and five younger siblings. We had a wonderful childhood and our home was always filled with laughter. Mum always used to bake on a Sunday and our Sunday night evening meal – or 'tea' as we used to call it – was like having a party, with cakes and jelly and custard.

Bobbie Binks was born in 1941 and grew up in Fazakerley, which is now seen as suburban but was then, like Huyton in the 1950s, on the outskirts of the countryside. His parents were Harry and Janet and he had two brothers, John, born in 1939, and Dave, who was born in 1943. Bobbie lived in Lower Lane; he remembers that:

> … there was a farm at the top end of the lane, where we used to go to see the animals. There was a big field of cows; my father used to send me down with a cart to collect all the cowpats. The rainwater was caught in a barrel and the cowpats added – and, boy! did the tomatoes in the greenhouse and the flowers grow! My father used to rear one turkey each year in the back garden to fatten it up for Christmas, along with a few chickens. We used to get upset when the time came to kill the birds, but we all had to take part in plucking the feathers in the kitchen.

But, even in the town, there were far more animals to be seen than there are today.

Alan Scott was born in 1952 and lived in Smithdown Lane:

> I lived directly opposite the Corporation yard and stables, which is now the location of the Mole of Edge Hill tunnels. I've got great memories of the shire horses used to pull the carts. My Granddad and his brother were both carters and Mr Holden, who was the Lord Mayor's coach driver, lived adjacent to the yards. We often saw the coach coming out for official duties. Police horses were also stabled there; it was great to see the mounted police in all their finery and hear the sound of the horse's hooves striking the cobbles. I remember once or twice that Roy Rogers' horse, Trigger, was stabled there during his visits to the city.
>
> Right next to the yard was a huge chimney stack, which was the exhaust for the fumes from the trains travelling in the tunnels from Edge Hill station to Lime Street. I could see the clock on the university Victoria building on Brownlow Hill from my bedroom window.
>
> The three-storey house we lived in was quite damp, the top floor just being used for storage. A coal fire was only ever lit in the living room. We had a front parlour, only used for special occasions; the door had a hook at the top so my brother and I couldn't get in; we'd use a brush handle to lift the hook and peek in; it was always spick and span.

*Elephants leaving Lime Street Station when the circus came to town!*

Barbara Walsh, *née* Mercer, grew up in Miranda Road, Kirkdale:

There was a blacksmith at the end of our road; the coalman had a horse and cart for his deliveries, as did many other businesses in those days. We rarely saw cars – the only one we saw was the landlord's when he came for the rent – he was the only person in the area who could afford one!

Agnes Jones, *née* Webb, also grew up in an area where there was plenty of life. Today, she lives in New Zealand but she recalls her time in Liverpool:

We lived in Park Lane, right in the centre of town in the tenements. Our flat was on the top landing and overlooked the docks. At that time, I hated living there and never let my friends at Central School know where I lived. However, looking back I can see that it was a friendly and safe community. St Vincent's RC Church was next door and the church bell pealed for Sunday mass right opposite our bedroom window. Nobody seemed to mind or moan about it.

Another comforting sound for me was the first tramcar rattling down the street in the early hours. I caught the No. 26 tram to school every day. The tramcars had an open platform on the top deck at the front and it was very daring to sit on that. On the journey home, there was a huge poster with 'Bovril for All Meat Dishes' on it. The illustration was of a big roast meal. I was so hungry that it made my mouth water!

Park Lane was extremely busy and we saw plenty of life from our top windows. A pub on the corner had its moments! And we could view all the brides who were married in St Vincent's. There was also a café, where Arab men sat all day, but they kept themselves to themselves.

Eileen Pritchard, *née* Smye, was born in 1944 and lived in Selwyn Street, Kirkdale:

We had gas lights in the house and there was great excitement when electricity was installed. We had a small concrete air-raid shelter in the garden, which was used to store garden tools until it was demolished.

Winters were cold with lots of snow and fog. I remember having to walk to and from school in the fog and snow. My bedroom window had ice on the inside in cold weather. I had seven blankets on my bed in order to keep warm and also my dad's army great-coat over the bed on very cold nights. I used to read books by torchlight under the bedclothes in order to keep warm and make my parents think I was asleep.

We could not afford a television until I was twelve. I was not allowed to switch it on until I had done my homework. It was a beautiful piece of furniture – a console with doors.

Eileen's extended family lived in the same street:

On Christmas Day I took my pillow-case full of toys to show all my relatives in the street. When I was about six I remember falling out with my mum and dad and filling a bag with all my dolls and teddies and going down the back entry saying I was going to live with my Auntie. I was there about twenty minutes before Dad came to find me!

Janet Arnot remembers the cosiness of life at home in Alderville Road:

This was in the days before central heating and in winter my dad used to light Valor stoves in the bedrooms and the toilet to warm them up. The Valor stove had a pattern of holes on the top and I used to love lying in bed and looking at the pattern, lit up on the ceiling, making a cosy glow. My memories of the house where I was actually born are vague.

The house that Janet barely remembers is the one in Stuart Road, Walton, where we, and our mum and dad, Ena and Alf Brown, lived from 1949 until 1956. I was four years old when we arrived from Maghull, and ten when we left.

I loved our house because it was exciting; it had a large attic and a cellar, with a coal cellar off it. Downstairs, there was a large front room with a marble fireplace. We didn't use this room a lot, but the piano was in there, so I went in most days to practice. There was a three-piece suite in soft brown velvet and, for some years, this was the only room with a carpet. The other rooms had home-made rag rugs or runners. There was a long hall with a dog-leg past the stairs, and halfway along it

*Janet Arnot, first school photograph, aged five.*

was the door to what we called the 'middle room'. It was a cosy room which we used in the winter because it was easier to heat. I remember lying on a drop-end sofa in this room when I had measles and whooping cough. The doctor, John McMaster, used to come often and he left me until the end of his round so that he could read me a story.

I remember my mother kneeling in front of the coal fire in that room one late winter's afternoon, melting a chocolate bar on a saucer and spreading it on the back of malted milk biscuits to tempt my convalescent appetite. Chocolate biscuits were pretty rare in 1950!

At the back of the house was a large kitchen with a big range, later replaced by my father with a wooden fireplace and mantelpiece. It isn't just childhood memory that makes me think that this was a large room, because there were two fireside chairs in it, my mother's sewing machine under the window, a large dresser-type sideboard and a kitchen table with six chairs round it. There was also a long airing rack suspended from the ceiling on a pulley.

I used to sit at the table in the evening drawing or 'colouring-in' while we listened to *The Archers*. My parents sat by the fireside, usually my mother would be knitting, but if a radio programme included dance music, especially a Strauss waltz, my parents would waltz around the room with plenty of space to turn. Off this kitchen was a scullery with the cooker, sink, draining board and the kitchen cabinet, a new acquisition in about 1952.

On the first floor, there were three large bedrooms. My parents had the front room which went across the whole width of the house. I had the middle bedroom, which, like all three bedrooms, had a little fireplace, where my mother lit a fire when I had whooping cough. These two bedrooms were up four stairs towards the front of the house from a half landing. On the front landing were the attic stairs, which turned on themselves on another small landing where there was a large built-in cupboard. This always reminded me of Enid Blyton's *Five Go Adventuring Again*, but no matter how much I tapped, no Secret Way appeared. My father had the attic as a workshop and, sometimes, after I was in bed, especially before Christmas, I would hear him moving about up there, or the sound of his saw.

Up two stairs towards the back of the house was the bathroom and toilet and, best of all, another large bedroom which I had for a playroom.

I was sad when we left this house for a smaller, more conventional one, but my mother had always missed having a garden. She had 'green fingers' and could grow anything.

Robin Bird, born in 1947, is another child who remembers moving house. He lived in Geraint Street, Liverpool. He remembers:

The household was dad, Bob, mother, Thea, elder sister Erica, plus my father's younger brothers, who lived with us for some reason. One had been demobbed from the Army. The house was two-up, two-down, which must have been cramped but did not feel it in my younger years. I remember the yard, the outside toilet, the cooking range and getting bathed in the earthenware sink.

Dad was a press photographer, with a photo booth in New Brighton, so we were the only ones in the street with a car, a pre-war Morris, which he later crashed and replaced with an Austin A35. We had the first television in the street too, and the front room was packed with neighbours for the Coronation in 1953. I believed it to be an important event, but I was disappointed that Muffin the Mule did not appear.

I had grandparents in Kensington and Seacombe, whom we visited. On reflection, we had a traditional household of two adults and two children, plus Dad's brothers. Then another baby sister came along. Geraint Street must have become too cramped and when I was about ten, we moved to Wallasey, as Dad had opened a photographic studio and we lived behind it. The thing that struck me most about Wallasey was that the river was at the bottom of the road. You could see the ships coming in and out as opposed to seeing them at the Landing Stage or in Liverpool Docks. Also, all the churches in Wallasey seemed small compared to the Cathedral, our local church. After moving over the river, I still went to school in Liverpool and cycled through the Birkenhead Tunnel every day.

Harold Russell was born in 1938 and most of his childhood was spent in Clubmoor. His first home was in Farrer Street but he later came to live at No.190, Townsend Lane, which he refers to as 'the Family House': 'I think of this house as a birthday present because my parents, Frank and Lilian, were given the keys to it on my fifth birthday.' Harold's brother, David Russell, my husband, was born in the front bedroom of this house in December 1945.

Chris Brocklehurst was born in 1939 in Liverpool's dockland, but his family moved to a tenement building in 1940 and this is the family home that he remembers:

My mother and father, Patrick and Catherine Brocklehurst, were always known as Paddy and Kitty Brock and we were known as the Brock family. In my family there were fourteen children plus Mum and Dad and an uncle who lived with us. We lived in a four-bedroomed flat in St Oswald's Street, Old Swan, where we had an inside bathroom, kitchen and back kitchen and a coal fire for heating the hot water. There was also a small fireplace in one bedroom and, if anyone was sick, they went in that bedroom. My dad was presented with a bravery award by Liverpool City Council when I was in my teens. He tried to save two small children from a fire in the tenements where we lived.

*Liverpool Cathedral, 1950s.*

Chris remembers his parents working hard for their large family:

My dad had worked on the docks until he had an accident when he became a 'Jack of all Trades' –

painter, decorator, joiner, cobbler – you name it, he could do it! Later, he became caretaker of St Oswald's Street School and was there until he retired. This was the school that I attended. My mother was always there for us. Yet she would also go to the school to clean and scrub the floors and, in the summer holidays, she and the other cleaners would wash all the walls and tiles down.

Ann Cowley was born in 1948 and lived in Hornby Street off Scotland Road. She recalls:

> It was a poor area but everyone had jobs in our street. There were factories, the docks, shops and many other types of employment. There was only the money lender who had a carpet; the rest of us in the street just had a small rug in front of the fireplace. Televisions were only starting to become available but nobody in our street had one. They were for the rich. But even though we were poor, I still had a happy childhood.
>
> I have lots of memories of those days and most of them are good ones. One of my first memories as a child in the fifties was listening to Dan Dare on the radio. I was about five years old but it was so exciting. I imagined what walking on the planet Mars would be like.

Shirley Evans, *née* Wilson, born in 1939, grew up in July Road with her parents, Frank and Mabel, and Frank, her younger brother:

> Our house was a terraced house with three bedrooms, although we didn't have a bathroom or inside toilet. My grandparents lived just four doors away in the same road, so I got to spend a lot of time with them too. My dad worked for British Rail on the delivery wagons, delivering parcels between stations and warehouses. He would work hard – twelve hours a day from 7 a.m. to 7 p.m. – and he would still help Mum with the housework.
>
> I wore lots of 'hand-me-downs' and homemade dresses and when the sales were on, Mum used to measure our feet by drawing round them on card, cutting the shapes out and taking them with her for our shoes. We played a lot of cards at home, mostly rummy, and my granddad loved to play dominoes. He taught me how to play Threes and Fives, which was also good practice for my maths. My granddad also used to make 'rag-rugs'. My job was to cut up the fabric – old coats and skirts mostly – into strips. Granddad would draw pictures on the back of the rug sacking, so that when they were completed they turned out well.

*Shirley Evans with her mother, Mabel.*

Threes and Fives are played with a standard domino set and some players use a cribbage board to keep track of the scoring.

Linda Leaworthy, *née* Lewis, was born in 1954. She lived in a police house in Bentley Road, Birkenhead with her parents, Stan and Vera, and her sisters, Christine and Diane. She remembers

> The only heat in the house was a coal fire in the living room and I can often remember ice on the inside of my bedroom window. The fire wasn't lit until we got home from school so we got dressed standing around the oven. We had lino on all the floors and a pulley in the kitchen to dry clothes on and the front room wasn't furnished until I was ten, but we did have an inside toilet, unlike my grandparents, Ada and William Lewis. When we went there we had to go down the yard to an outside toilet.
>
> My clothes were made by my mum and I only had my school uniform, playing-out clothes and a dress for Sunday School. My dad always cut my hair and he mended our shoes. He made us a chair out of a barrel which my mum padded and covered in material. I still have it and my grand-daughter sits in it.

The children of the 1950s were the first generation who experienced the welfare state, including the infant health service, from the beginning of their lives. Linda continues:

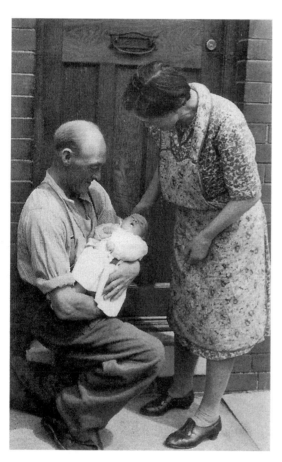

*Linda Leaworthy with her grandparents;*
*Ada and William Lewis.*

> I was in hospital quite a lot when I was little and, unlike today, when your mum can stay with you, my mum could only visit twice a week. My sisters used to come to the top of the hill near the hospital and wave to me because I don't think they were allowed to visit. The ward sister was quite strict and we had to behave. We always got hot milk to drink before bed and everyone hated it. I still can't drink it!

Pat Gilbert, living in Bootle, remembers:

> When I was fourteen, my mum had a baby in hospital. They dressed me up in a camel coat with a big collar and this vile brown feathered hat in order to get in to see my mum and new baby sister. They didn't allow children in to visit in those days!

Christine McGarry, *née* Harrison, was born in June 1947 and lived in West Derby. She reminisces:

> We had a black telephone in the hall with what was known as a party line; this meant that you shared the line with another family. Sometimes you'd

*Linda Leaworthy, second child from the left, with her back to the camera in St Catherine's Hospital.*

pick the phone up and hear someone on the line talking. There were few people with phones in those days so quite often neighbours would ask to use the phone but they'd always leave a couple of coppers to cover the cost. In fact, one neighbour, called Mrs Grogan, had a cake shop over on Larkhill Lane and she used to come to phone in her order. Imagine running a business without a phone these days! Mrs Grogan lived next door but one and she was typical of the neighbourliness that abounded in those days. We were in and out of each other's houses and even though she didn't have a telephone, she had a TV – a tiny little brown box affair – and we all squeezed in to watch the Coronation on it. We got beautiful china cups and saucers to commemorate the occasion but I have no idea what happened to them.

# 2

# CLEANLINESS IS NEXT TO GODLINESS!

Mary Parkin lived in Roscommon Street in a house that still had the disadvantages of the Edwardian period, as well as some of its surviving beauty:

> There was no bathroom and all we had was a stone sink in the back kitchen with a brass cold water tap. We washed by boiling kettles and having 'cat-licks', as my nana called them, until we could have a bath at the public baths once a week. Everything was washed in that sink: hand-washing, the dishes, us! We used Lifebuoy soap to wash us and Fairy, which was green, or Sunlight soap, which was yellow, to wash any clothes or even the dishes. I had my hair washed in Derbac soap, which was black and guaranteed to get rid of any head-lice. Should any escape, Mum used to comb my hair every week with a metal comb over a newspaper to catch any livestock! If any were found, they were burned in the kitchen fire. Of course, there was always the visit from the dreaded 'nit nurse', who came into school to examine our heads regularly and excluded anyone who was found to have a 'dirty head'.
>
> We visited the public baths to get a proper bath. You usually went with a friend to the 'Washallovers', taking a towel and some soap with you. The baths were in tiled cubicles, which were just partitions and not at all sound-proof. The attendant would have fitted well into the army and was probably a direct descendant of Attila the Hun! You had to wait your turn and then you were called into the cubicle. The attendant had filled the bath with really hot water and she went out and shut the door, telling you not to be long! There was no way we could cool the temperature of the water as she had the big key which turned the tap on and off, which she took with her. It took you all your time to sit down in the water; you took turns with your friend to sit at the brass tap end because that was hot as well! The bath was cleaned between 'guests' with Vim and so, at the bottom, it was always gritty. By the time it was cool enough to sit down, the attendant was banging on the door telling you to get out! Everyone came out with red legs and very red bums!

Moira Kennedy, *née* Fitzsimmons, was born in 1942 in St Asaph, where her mother had been evacuated. After the war, she grew up in Exley Street, behind the Grafton Rooms on West Derby Road:

> We used Margaret Street Public Baths to bathe – no hot tap in our house. Dad's shirts went to the Chinese laundry to be cleaned and collars to be starched. I took washing to the launderette for Mum and also for the lady next door, who gave me half a crown and I felt rich!

Alan Scott lived in Smithdown Road. He too has memories of the public baths:

> We had no hot water, the only cold tap being in the kitchen over a porcelain sink; the toilet was at the bottom of the yard, which was a long cold walk in the dark of night with only a candle for company, beyond the brick-built air-raid shelter. My brother and I would go to the public baths in Minshull Street every Saturday morning and share a hot bath.

*The wash house was an important facility and meeting place in 1950s' Liverpool: Claire Street wash house, 1956.*

Alan's mother was a regular user of the wash house:

> Mum would trudge along with other women later in the day to the adjoining wash house, all the women pushing prams full of washing, or carrying big bundles on their heads, to spend a couple of hours washing, drying and ironing.

Eileen Pritchard lived in Selwyn Street, Kirkdale:

> We had no bathroom – we had a bath once a week in the tin bath before the fire in the living room. My mum did not like me inviting friends to stay as she was embarrassed about not having a bathroom. They eventually turned one of the bedrooms into a bathroom after I had left home. We had to go the full length of the backyard to the toilet, which used to freeze up in the winter. We had to put our coats on if it was raining and take a brolly.

Mary Parkin recalls the outside facilities in her Roscommon Street home:

> We had a big backyard, which was whitewashed from time to time. Dad would get big blocks of lime and put them in an enamel bucket with water to make the whitewash to paint on the walls. We had an outside toilet with a scrubbed wooden seat and we used a candle at night to go outside because there wasn't an outside light. Toilet paper was pieces of newspaper torn up and put on a string. It wasn't until later in my childhood that we had 'proper' toilet paper. The backyard joined onto another toilet which belonged to two families in the next street and they used a key to gain access to their loo; at least we had the luxury of one of our own!

Shelagh Nugent remembers the agonies of having long hair and a vivid imagination!

> In the kitchen there was a gas boiler. The boiler was for laundry and heating washing-up water. The sink was one of those old stone things and the draining board was wooden. It used to get slimy and wet and had to be scrubbed fiercely with Vim. I used to lie on the draining board and have my long hair washed in the sink. It was torture. I don't know why they insisted on long hair. If washing was bad, the biddy comb was unnecessary cruelty.
>
> We didn't have the luxury of indoor plumbing, so upstairs it was a chamber pot under the bed. This was known as the jerry, perhaps because it was shaped a bit like a German tin hat. It was my mum's job to empty the jerries. She got all the best jobs!
>
> At the bottom of the yard was the toilet. It was no fun sitting there on a cold dark night waiting for Spring-Heeled Jack to leap over the wall and rip your throat out. Honestly, life was just full of peril in those days!

Janet Arnot, born in 1952, had a less perilous lifestyle. She says:

> I was four when we moved into the house off Walton Hall Avenue that I grew up in. The toilet was off the back porch, so my dad moved the door so that the toilet was inside the house. Moving the back door to bring the lavatory indoors was one of the first improvements that my father tackled when we arrived in Alderville Road.

In the 1950s, many families survived and kept scrupulously clean in circumstances which did not offer much comfort, and certainly not the level of enjoyment and relaxation that people expect to find in modern bathrooms. The idea of having a shower every morning and then, perhaps, bathing or showering again in the evening was unimaginable luxury. Hair was washed once a week – a television commercial of the time announced: 'Friday Night is Amami Night.' Amami was a setting lotion! Candles were lit in bathrooms or toilets because there was no other lighting, not to create an ambience.

Hazel Skarratts, *née* Unwin, born in 1943, lived in Uldale Close, Norris Green. She remembers how families shared those benefits that came their way:

> I come from a family of six children. My father was an upholsterer and my mother was a cleaner in Ellergreen Road School. Our house was quite posh, because we had a bath, although it was off the back-kitchen. Most of my dad's family lived in Bootle and they would call in and have a bath!

Pauline Bennett, *née* Green, lived in Sunningdale Road, Liverpool 15, moving to Sandown Road in December 1956, when she was twelve. The Greens were a happy family: with older sister, Sheila, younger twins, Bernard and Carol, born in 1947; and the youngest, Brenda, born in 1954.

Pauline remembers the hard work, but also the cosiness of life at home:

> Mum was always up first and would say, 'Stay in bed until I light the fire'. In the winter, we could write our names in the ice on the inside of the windows. Bath time was Friday night. When Brenda was born in 1954, she slept in a drawer that had been taken from the dressing table and lined with a blanket.
>
> The weekly wash was done at the wash house, with lots of items also being ironed there. The washing was taken in a wash basket and pushed in an old pushchair. Mum always stopped at the butcher's to pick up some meat for the dinner. The wash house would be frowned on today, but many families used the facilities. It enabled large amounts of laundry to be washed, dried and ironed, if needed.

Mary Parkin's mother also used the wash house:

> Mum took our washing to the wash house on Netherfield Road. She took all the dirty clothes and put them on an old pram to carry them more easily. She wore wellies and a rubber apron. I used to go up there after a certain amount of time and help her fold the clothes. She did the hand-washing in a 'stall', which was a small cubicle with a sink and hot and cold water and a draining-board made of wood which she used to put the clothes on to scrub. After she had washed and rinsed the clothes, she would put them through a huge mangle. I often had to help retrieve the clothes as they came through from the other end. The sheets and towels were put into huge washing machines. The wet clothes were then put on the maidens, which were enormous drying chambers. Hard to describe, but there were rails, on which the wet clothes were put, which were pulled out of the wall. When they were full of clothes, these were pushed back and the heat would dry the clothes. They were very heavy and the heat in the wash house was terrific!
>
> When they were dry, the clothes would be rolled out through huge rollers to press them and then I would help Mum fold them to be brought home. The iron that we used originally was a flat iron which was put on the fire to get hot. We ironed on the table with an old blanket and sheet on top. We used to keep putting the iron back on the heat as it quickly got cold. You had to keep spitting on it to test how hot it was! I didn't have a lot of clothes and we wore things for much longer before they were washed than children do today. When I got my school uniform for Queen Mary High School in 1957, I got two blouses and three pairs of knickers and they lasted all week until they were washed at the weekend.

Bill Duvall recalls:

> My granddad sold soap powder outside the wash house in Lodge Lane until the mid-sixties. My dad worked in the baths as a boiler-man so we got in free. We often went to the baths – they had some kind of oblong tiled tubs that the public used. Carbolic soap is still one I use from time to time even now; this always takes me back. In those days we had no running hot water in the house; it was a two-up, two-down.

The public wash house and public bath house system owed its origins to Kitty Wilkinson, born Catherine Seaward in Ireland in 1786. Her parents set out to bring Kitty and her sister to Liverpool for a better life, but they were shipwrecked on the voyage and Kitty's mother and sister were drowned. Somehow, she and her father survived together in Liverpool; from the age of ten, Kitty was employed, first to run messages, then in service and, later, she moved to Caton, near Lancaster, to work in a mill. Kitty married a seaman, but was left a widow with two small children when he was lost at sea. Kitty returned to Liverpool, where she took in washing in order to earn a living. She married Tom Wilkinson and settled down to life in Denison Street. In 1832, there was an outbreak of cholera in Liverpool and Kitty offered her boiler, the only one in the street, to her neighbours for laundering infected clothes and bed-linen. The project was so well managed and so much needed that it led to the establishment of the first public wash house in the country. In 1846, Kitty and Tom were made the first superintendents of the public baths in Frederick Street, which were the first in Liverpool and, indeed, in the country. Kitty's foresight, courage and Christian charity are commemorated in a window in Liverpool's Anglican Cathedral, along with other 'Noble Women' of the city.

# 3

# SHOPPING AND EATING

Peacetime appeared gradually in some ways; for instance, rationing did not end in September 1945 with Victory in Japan (VJ) Day, as some people had expected, and the children of the early fifties were well acquainted with rationing.

There was resentment when rationing continued for so long after the end of the Second World War. People had expected an immediate improvement in their conditions after victory was achieved. This did not happen; in fact, bread was rationed from 1946 until 1948. The allowances varied for men and women, manual workers, adolescents, children and infants. Potatoes were also rationed from autumn 1947 until April 1948. This disappointment was made worse for those who had come through the hardships of wartime by the knowledge that their erstwhile enemies were being given assistance to stabilise their countries, while Britain was still paying off debts to the United States for weapons that had been vitally needed to continue the lone fight against Nazi oppression. The lend-lease debt to the United States was finally cleared in 2006.

In the early 1950s, however, people were outwardly stoical in their attitudes and children knew nothing other than rationing.

Pauline Bennett was still only six years old in October 1950, but clearly remembers her ration book; as it was not until 1954 that fourteen years of rationing came to an end, when meat and bacon came off ration. In May 1950, rationing ended for canned and dried fruit, chocolate biscuits, treacle, syrup, jellies and mincemeat. Tea was rationed until 1952, and tea leaves were often used at least twice in most homes. Tea bags were virtually unknown at this time. In 1953, there was an end to sugar rations, but, by this time, some people had become so used to sugarless drinks that they never took sugar again. Others made up for lost time and took at least two spoonfuls for the rest of their lives. Egg rationing also ended in 1953. Eggs had not always been rationed, but neither were they always available in towns. In 1954, cheese came off ration, making it easier for housewives to provide 'carry-out' lunches. Of course, for most people, cheese meant Cheddar, Cheshire, perhaps Red Leicester, or unspecified, white, red or 'mousetrap'. More exotic varieties were much more expensive and obtainable only at certain shops, such as Cooper's Store in Church Street.

Rationing meant that people were careful with food and there was very little waste. Betty Duncan was at school in the early fifties, when many items were still rationed. She recalls:

> I was more interested in Sciences and did not do well at cookery or needlework. When everyone else made a Christmas cake, I cleaned a cooker because Miss Thomas, the cookery mistress, said that she couldn't allow me to waste all those good ingredients!

Pauline remembers:

> Grocery shopping was done in Hamilton's on Picton Road; you queued and were served. They had flip-top tins with a selection of biscuits. You could buy a pound of mixed biscuits, asking for more of your favourites. Broken biscuits were cheaper.

Broken biscuits were usually called 'brokes' and were often bought for children.
Pauline continues:

Bacon, cheese and some other items were from the Maypole; butter was cut off a block and patted into shape, then wrapped. Fruit and vegetables were from Hargreaves. My mum had to make two trips for fruit and veg alone, for the weekend. Sometimes we went with her and helped. Bread was bought daily from the nearby shop; this was baked locally and bought unwrapped.

The Maypole was a long-established chain, with its origins in the early nineteenth century, when it was exclusively the Maypole Dairies. But, in the early 1950s, many shops were family-run and independent of any large organisation.

Milk was delivered by the local dairy via horse and cart. The dairy was in a built-up area opposite our school and had cows kept there. Occasionally, we bought sarsaparilla, delivered in stone jars.

Blocks of ice were delivered to the local fish and chip shop; the blocks of ice were pulled off the vehicle onto the floor and we scurried to pick up chunks of ice to suck.

I still have my ration book and remember going to the sweet shop and them cutting out the coupon.

When sweet rationing ended on 5 February 1953, many adults were just as thrilled as the children, so there was always the hope that, besides pocket-money sweets, generous fathers might bring home a box of chocolates to be shared whilst listening to the radio or watching TV in the evening. But children were not used to demanding sweets or treats, and many were quite amazed by Rowntree's advertising catchphrase showing a child calling, 'Don't forget the Fruit Gums, Mum!' For them, this would have guaranteed no sweets that day!

Joe Swindells remembers the end of sweet rationing:

Although most kids only got a bit of pocket money, the sweet shop was a favourite haunt for all the kids, especially on a Saturday when we got our pocket money – in our case, the princely sum of 1s. But what you could get for that! My brother and I would buy our favourite comics – the Dandy and the Beano. We could always swap these with our friends for the Knockout, Film Fun, Topper, Beezer or Lion.

Then there was the vast array of mouth-watering sweets. You were spoilt for choice! Some of the most popular that I used to buy were Refreshers or Love Hearts because they were fizzy like Kali Lumps. Spangles had a variety of flavours, like Acid Drop, Fruit Flavour and Humbug. Then there were Black Jacks, Victory V lozenges, Fruit Gums and Pastilles, Pear Drops, Pineapple Chunks, Cream Soda, Sherbet Lemons and Sherbet Fountains, Gobstoppers, Sticky Lice (Liquorice Root), Barley Sugar Twist, Arrow Bars and all kinds of chewing

*Children loved the various flavours of Spangles at pocket-money prices.*

gum, like Beech Nut, and bubblegum, like Chix. Usually we would buy two ounces of something from the many jars on the shelves.

Janet Dalton has a special reason to remember the sort of dairy that Pauline Bennett mentions:

> I was brought up in Walton near Walton Hospital and my father was a cow keeper and ran a dairy business from our house. The house was on the end of terrace and had been built as a 'milk house' to serve milk to the surrounding houses. Behind the house was a large two-storey cow shed for the thirty cows we kept. The cows were in the lower storey and were milked there. Above was a store for feed for the cows. In the middle of the large yard stood the midden that held all the manure. As a child, I just accepted this, but now I wonder what the neighbours thought of it all. When the midden was cleared on alternate weeks by two farmers from Melling and Kirkby, the true aromas of the countryside could be appreciated in Walton.
>
> Because our house had such a large yard at the back, it was an excellent place for our friends to play. We would dress up in our mothers' clothes and have concerts and impromptu Rose Queen parades. My sister's favourite was to arrange the milk crates into a show-jumping arena and we would jump over these crates with skipping ropes tied around us as reins.
>
> My father employed three men who looked after the cows and bottled all the milk. Schoolboys pushing handcarts delivered the milk before they went to school.
>
> The house also incorporated a small shop which my mother looked after. Customers came in to pay the milk bill and the shop sold eggs and general provisions as well as milk. I enjoyed working in the shop but the real treat was to go with my father when he bought cows from markets in Cheshire and Yorkshire, and, best of all, when we went to the agricultural shows – the Christmas Show at Stanley Cattle Market on Prescot Road, and the shows at Liverpool, Formby and Woolton. I sat up on the cattle wagon with the driver, and joy was complete if my father won a prize for the cows he was showing.

Hazel Rimmer, *née* Hall, lived in Ruskin Street, Walton, where her father, Edward, had a dairy:

> My father had his own cows, which were kept in a shippen. They had to be milked morning and night; before the morning milking he would deliver milk to his customers, so he rose at about 5 a.m. I liked nothing better than to go into the shippen and it was always exciting when the calves were born.
>
> My mum, Winifred, did not go out to work, but she worked very hard helping Dad, serving the customers who didn't have their milk delivered. The shop also sold ice-cream and sweets. I loved helping in the shop.

Madeleine Roberts, *née* Chisnall, born in 1946, lived in Kirkby, where her parents kept a shop on Glover's Brow, near the railway station:

> I lived in Kirkby during the 1950s; it was a village at that time and didn't have many amenities. My parents worked in a local shop, a newsagent's, on the main road. After a while, the owner of the shop built a new shop next door to the newsagent's that my parents ran as a grocery shop. These were among the first shops in the area. My dad used to deliver orders to people who lived around; it wasn't just groceries, he would take other things if they asked for them. My parents worked full-time in the shop so my granddad looked after us; he lived with us. I remember enjoying egg and chips and scouse and, when I went to a school-friend's house for tea, we had fried spam and chips – it was lovely!

Hazel Skarratts remembers her mother as a wonderful manager:

Mother was a very good cook and, with having six children, she had to make her money go as far as she could; she would make scouse, liver and onions, potted herrings, bacon ribs – all good food. On a Sunday, she would make egg custard, scones and apple pies. You wouldn't have a choice and had to eat what you were given; if you didn't like it, you had bread and jam. When we were about thirteen, we would go over the water to Moreton, cockling. My mam would soak the cockles overnight and, next morning, boil them with porridge oats to get all the sand out. Then we would wait for them to go cold and eat them with vinegar. We would do our shopping daily because we didn't have a fridge; when my mam made a jelly, she would put it in the backyard and put a plate on with a big brick on to stop the cats getting it.

Margaret Dunford, born on 31 January 1947, lived in Norris Green from the age of six months. She recalls:

Rationing went on until 1953, but we did not notice because it was all we knew. My mam would say, 'I am going for my rations' when going shopping, but we were well fed, although I was one of six. We would eat scouse, corned beef hash, rabbit stew; cakes were mostly homemade but we only seemed to have them on Sunday teatime with jelly and custard. I loved school dinners but only had them when my dad was on strike on the docks, because they were free then – lovely cheese pie and mash, and sponge and custard. We would walk to Strawberry Road near Broadway for school dinner – it was about fifteen minutes' walk from school.

I also loved the lolly-ice man coming down the road on his bike, ringing a bell. I used to get a penny spearmint lolly. I remember Taylor's bread-cart with the horse, but the coalman had a lorry. It was hard work for the women; lighting the fire before they got you up for school and then they had to make the porridge. I don't remember cereals then.

Janet Arnot has vivid early memories of the shop, Swift's Stores, in Stuart Road, Walton:

I remember the grocer's shop next door to us. It was run by a man called Charlie. I remember the big red bacon slicer and the way the slices curled off the sides of bacon and slithered into a neat pile on the grease-proof paper laid on the tray. In those days, cheese came in a large wheel that stood on a cool slab at one end of the counter; whenever my mother carried me into the shop, Charlie would cut a wedge of cheese from the wheel and give it to me. I'm told I ate cheese before anything else and it's still a favourite.

This shop was a local social centre, where people met and exchanged news, partly because of Charlie's cheerful and friendly nature, but also his kindly wife, Mrs McDougall, always called 'Mrs Mac', and the assistants, Mary and Muriel, who knew everyone and were both well liked by the customers. In the morning, when Charlie unhooked the two tall wooden doors from the porch at the front of the shop, they were placed in our front garden leaning against the wall of the shop.

When Charlie was very busy, or one of the assistants was unwell, my mother used to 'weigh up' the butter and lard, currants, raisins, sultanas and sugar on our kitchen table, so that customers would not be kept waiting in the shop. Charlie would carry the heavy scales in and put them on the table with all the brass weights; then he would carry in whatever item he needed to be weighed. The butter and lard were wrapped in squares of grease-proof paper and the dried fruit and sugar went into stiff dark blue paper bags. My mother became very good at gauging the weights by sight and this was important as people did not like 'bitty' packages of lard, or, particularly, butter. We had a special feeling of connection with 'our' shop and, at Christmas, Charlie used our big dining table to store all the special orders of tins of biscuits, boxes of chocolates and selection boxes, all with labels bearing the names of the purchasers. This made Christmas seem even more exciting! Payment for my mother's help was in kind – some of the goods that she had been weighing and, at Christmas, a fancy tin of biscuits. We loved these tins with the pictures on the top of winter scenes or flowers, and used them to keep Plasticine, chalks or various 'treasures' that we had collected.

Janet continues:

> Mum kept a large jar of Malt Extract on top of the kitchen cabinet and gave us a spoonful regularly, which I loved. Whenever she made rice pudding, my sister and I would take turns over who would have the nutmeg 'toffee' on the top. I used to enjoy helping make cakes with my mum. Whenever I was ill and had lost my appetite, she would give me a peeled orange and some sugar in a saucer to dip it in.

Janice Pickthall, née Gabriel, was born in 1947. She recounts:

> I was born and bred in Walton in a two-up, two-down house in Kiddman Street, off Breeze Hill. We knew all the neighbours, calling them Mr, Mrs or Miss and all the children by their names. My mum didn't go to work and did lots of sewing, making me dresses out of my sister's 'cast-offs'; she also did lots of cooking and baking. We used to shop at the row of shops on Breeze Hill; they were Beresford's fish shop, Parry's haberdashery, the chippy, the pub, Edna Jones the hairdresser, Lambert's butchers, Morris's Toys and the Gentlemen's Barber. They were demolished in the 1960s to make way for the fly-over at the Queen's Drive and Rice Lane junction. It was sad to see them go!

Charles Griffiths' grandmother, Mrs Green, owned the fish shop on Breeze Hill. Charles remembers:

> The shop was shut for some years, although my grandmother still lived at No. 30 Breeze Hill. I went to the Liverpool Collegiate School in 1952 and I remember getting off the bus at Walton Church and walking to Breeeze Hill to meet my mother, who would do her shopping along County Road on Tuesdays and Fridays and then call on my grandmother. I would go to carry my mother's shopping bags home for her. She would have bought the Children's Newspaper for us at the sweet shop next door to the butcher's shop. There were a couple of pubs along that stretch of Breeze Hill, one of which was The Peveril on the corner of Peveril Street.

Mary Allport, née McAteer, born in 1941, lived in Queens Road, Bootle. She recalls:

> As children we used to go down to the big warehouses and ask the dockers to put their hooks in the big bags of sugar and fill up our tins with this wonderful brown sugar. I also remember going to school taking a National Dried Milk tin and getting cocoa and sugar as a treat.
>
> On the corner of Derby Road and Bedford Place, there used to be a big bakery called Blackledges. We went to the back door on a Sunday and they used to sell us broken cakes and barm cakes for only coppers. That's as near as we got to shop-bought cakes.
>
> There was a lady in the house opposite to us, who used to make toffee apples – threepence for one, sixpence for a double-decker – they tasted wonderful!

John Halley remembers shopping with his mother:

> In those days, shops were closed on Wednesday afternoon and on Sunday. There was no pre-packed food – everything was fresh from all the different shops – butcher, baker, grocer, fish-monger – bacon from the bacon slicer and butter cut from a slab and, as a treat, a fresh rabbit from the butcher meant rabbit pie or rabbit stew. Mmm!

Not all memories of food are pleasant ones. Shelagh Nugent recalls her nan's 'waste not, want not' approach:

When the milk went sour, which happened frequently as we had no fridge, my nan would wait until it was solid and then plop it into a muslin bag and hang it over the sink to drain off the whey. She called it cottage cheese. It was revolting and smelled even worse than it tasted!

My nan was responsible for all the cooking as my mum worked full-time for Littlewood's Pools. As soon as I was old enough to reach the top of the cooker, I started to take over the catering duties so my nan could concentrate on her Woodbines and the reading of cowboy books. I could cook a full roast dinner well before I left primary school.

Eileen Pritchard lived in Selwyn Street, Kirkdale, and remembers the days when whole extended families lived near each other and children enjoyed the benefits of this arrangement:

Lots of my relatives lived in the same street and used to be popping in and out of each other's houses, often sharing a stew or an apple pie. My grandma used to decorate the most amazing birthday cakes, which were hidden from me in the front parlour until the day of my birthday! One thing that was important was remembering Mum's Co-op number when I went for the shopping – 182787.

The Co-operative movement grew from one shop in Rochdale, and, at its peak, there were 30,000 shops. One of the reasons for its success and popularity was the dividend or 'divvy' that it paid to its members from the trading profits. In order to receive the correct 'divvy', the customer had to give in their number when buying at the Co-op. Most children, growing up in the 1950s, knew their mother's Co-op number by heart, because they were often sent 'on a message'. At the beginning of the decade, very few families had refrigerators and some had irregular incomes, so shopping was often done 'little and often' with children being sent to the main Co-op for small amounts of perishables like bacon, or to the Co-op dairy for milk.

Sometimes Co-op numbers were inherited – my mother's number had been that of her own mother. When my mother began to keep house for her father and brother, she used the family Co-op number – 124068. The care that was taken, in always remembering and quoting the Co-op number when shopping, shows how important the 'divvy' was to families who budgeted carefully, and to whom thrift was one of the main virtues that kept your family out of debt and worry.

Chris Brocklehurst remembers eating good, plain food:

Most of our meals were basic. Sunday's left-overs, if there were any, would be made into Monday's tea. Shopping was done on Prescot Road at Irwin's or the Maypole. There were shops under St Oswald's House and Gardens, where most of the other shopping was done; Waterworth's for vegetables, Whiteway was the chemist and Sykes for bread, cheese and eggs. My mother was a good customer of the local pawn shop, where my dad's suit would go in on a Monday and, hopefully, out on a Friday! I remember the ration books and, when one of my younger sisters was born, my mother got dried milk in tins, and orange juice that you had to dilute, from the Clinic in Rathbone Road, where she was also given cod liver oil in a small bottle.

Shirley Evans' mother also shopped at Irwin's:

Mum shopped at Irwin's grocery store twice a week, doing a large shop on a Friday and a small one on a Tuesday. I don't ever remember being hungry, so Mum must have managed well. On Saturdays, I also did shopping for Mum, Gran and a neighbour for which I would get 1s 6d, which I saved for Christmas presents and holidays.

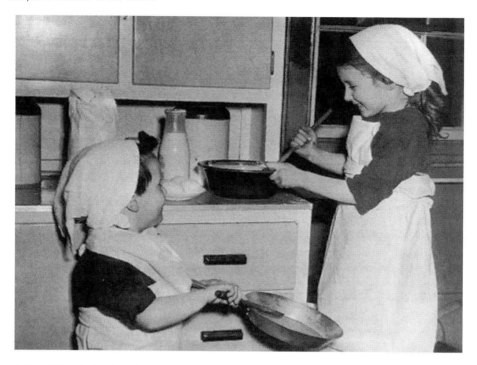

*Robin and Erica Bird celebrate Pancake Day (Shrove Tuesday). The photograph appeared in the Liverpool Echo.*

Robin Bird remembers: 'making pancakes with my sister, Erica, at Geraint Street. Our father, photographer Bob Bird, recorded the moment for the *Liverpool Echo*. I recall that the kitchen cabinet was in the classic fifties' colour scheme of green and cream!'

Bill Duvall remembers crowded mealtimes in the terraced house where he lived with his large extended family:

> Mealtimes in a two-up, two-down terrace house with up to thirteen people were very cramped. Mum, Dad and Granddad sat at the table; we older children sat on the stairs in tier fashion. Grown-ups ate different food from children in those days – or maybe it was just in our house – chips or soup was our main diet with plenty of bread. School meals were free; even in the school holidays we would go to school to have our dinner. Other kids from other schools were also there and usually this would end in a fight. However, we all enjoyed our meals and they did us no lasting harm – me and my brothers are all about 6ft tall!

Alan Scott remembers shopping with his grandma:

> I was looked after by my paternal grandma as a toddler, prior to school age, and she took me all over the city. I have some great memories of St John's Market and Coopers on Church Street. She often took me to town to the old St John's Market, where we would have a cup of tea and a toasted teacake, which, to me, as a toddler, seemed huge. I remember the cobbles of the fish market, sloped to the middle where the gutters were, and the grand entrance of the market where there was a butcher's right next to it. I also remember going to Coopers on Church Street, where Gran bought fresh butter from a barrel and the speed at which the staff would paddle it into a rectangular block and wrap it in grease-proof paper. We used to get the tram all the way from the Pier Head to Huyton and get off at the Eagle & Child to walk through to Greenway Square. I still recall the noise

of the trams: a slow click-clack, a continuous rumbling trundling grinding, the squeal of the brakes as the driver spun the brake wheel and the occasional crack of a spark from the overhead lines.

Mary Parkin remembers shopping in Scotland Road:

I used to do 'messages' down at the Co-op and can still remember my mum's divvy number – 176906. I also shopped at Pegrams in Scotland Road and can remember that the sugar came in blue paper bags and butter was wrapped in grease-proof paper. I remember going to the sweet shop with a coupon when sweet rationing was still in place. I would inevitably lose the coupon and she began to give me the ration book to take with me.

We ate a lot of offal – liver, kidneys, heart – and, of course, scouse. Nana made brawn and cowheel soup and we ate trotters and pig's feet and pickled herrings. Mum ate pig's belly, which was the stomach of a pig, but different from belly pork and chitterlings, which, I think, were pig's intestines. If we had a joint of beef on Sunday, the fat was used to make dripping toast with salt on which you had for supper. We always had a cooked meal each night and if we were peckish later on, Dad would make a pan of chips with beef dripping! Mum baked meat pies and apple pies, but she didn't make cakes, although when she started to work in Jacob's biscuit factory, she brought home mis-shapes on a regular basis.

Saturdays, we bought 'kewins' from the fish shop that, I think, were winkles. They were measured using a big enamel cup and when they were brought home they had to be boiled in a big pan and then eaten cold with a safety pin while listening to the wireless or, later on, watching television.

Jim Greer, born in 1935, lived in the Scotland Road area:

Our mother brought up eight children on a small income. She could make a meal out of anything. We all ate the same food. We had two sittings – the four oldest, then the four youngest. To help our mother, we'd go to Great Homer Street fruit market and collect the best fades from the bins and bring them home. Mother would cut out the faded parts and make apple pies. We used to sell our sweet coupons to better-off children, then get brown sugar from Bibby's and melt it in a tray. When it was nearly set, we'd criss-cross it.

Christine McGarry remembers the local shops:

I grew up in a Corporation house on Queen's drive, Liverpool. My nana's sister and family lived five doors away and my father's parents lived 'over the road' in Eastman Road. The grandfather I lived with had detachable shirt collars, which were sent to the laundry over by Larkhill shops. I particularly remember Clee's, which was a chandler's and I can still smell the creosote that pervaded the shop. We spent our pocket money at Crebbin's which was on the same block, buying four chews for a penny, a farthing for one, sherbet lemons which took the roof off your mouth, sherbet dabs – a yellow cylindrical container with a hard stick of liquorice peeking out of the top – twopenny toffee bars which we sucked until they softened and stretched, and, in hot weather, a Twicer which was an ice-cream lolly ice.

This was the well-known Liverpool-based Pendleton's Twicer, which had a memorable jingle: 'What could be nicer than a Pendleton's Twicer – Ice-cream with a lolly each end!'

Christine also recalls:

... a shop called Finvoys, which was past Maiden Lane, where you could buy a lolly ice on a wooden stick which, if you were really lucky, had a little brown mark on the stick which meant you got another lolly for free! Heaven!

Christine regularly shopped at the weekend:

> Pocket money was earned. I got sixpence every Saturday because I did the shopping. I would go to the Co-op over at Lark Hill shops on the Drive, armed with the shopping list for essentials like a quarter of Typhoo loose tea – later 99 tea, a quarter lb of butter, sugar, bread, etc. My mum always wrote her 'divvy' number at the top and I can still remember it – 119682! There were counters along three sides of the shop and you handed over the list and the assistant scurried around, getting all the items together, after which your money was placed in a metal container on a line-type conveyor and it whizzed up to a cashier who dispensed the change. I would struggle home with the shopping and then return to Waterworth's for the fruit and vegetables. There was a sweet shop a few doors up, run by a family called the Shuttleworths, who had one daughter called Cynthia. Next door was Clook's – the baker's – and we did have the occasional sausage roll. Our meals usually consisted of a chop or mince, peas and mashed potato. Chicken was a real luxury, whereas beef was commonplace. There was very little 'convenience food' – a trip to the chippie for chips and fish-cakes was a special treat. We were a Catholic family, so this was always on a Friday. We also had stews and scouse, as well as a Sunday roast. I remember thinking one of our neighbours was very posh because she had chicken on a Sunday!

David Russell also remembers this area:

> Our local shops were round the corner from Townsend Lane in Larkhill Lane. I remember shopping there with my mother. The funny thing is that I remember the order of the shops, starting from the furthest point. It could be that this was the way we did the shopping so that we did not have to carry the heavy bags too far, bearing in mind that Waterworth's, the greengrocer, was the furthest away.
>
> I remember the chandler's shop, where you could buy 'Aunt Sally' liquid to make bubbles. Then there was Waterworth's with the fascinating wooden bins set into the wall, holding the different varieties of potatoes. The potatoes were loaded into the top and cascaded, rumbling down onto a wooden tray at the bottom of each bin. Next in my memory comes the sweet shop, then the fishmonger, followed by Marshall and Weetch. Marshall and Weetch was where Mum bought biscuits and bacon. I'm sure that she bought other things as well, but I remember the tins of biscuits arrayed in a frame, each tin being twelve inches by twelve inches by twenty-four inches deep (I think) and one was always custard creams and the other 'brokes'. The other fascination in this shop was the bacon slicer, which was manually operated, shaving off rashers of bacon to the required thickness.
>
> Moving along the lane in my memory, we come to a small church; what denomination it was, I do not know. However, the intriguing thing here was that it had a glass case outside with an open Bible inside, with a different page open each time you went by.
>
> The Co-op came next. I don't know why, but, to me, it was an intimidating place. It could be that it was larger than the other shops, with a large wide counter. This made the staff further away and more aloof and, of course, there was the cashier sitting in the office looking down on the shop as the counter staff sent the money in cylinders along the wires. If you were sent to the Co-op on your own for a message you had to remember your mum's Co-op number – 164804 – it became imprinted on your mind. When you went on your own, you were ignored until all the grown-ups had been served – I think this was all part of the intimidated feelings I had.
>
> The Co-op dairy was in a different shop around the corner in Malleson Road. We went in there to buy our milk tickets each week.
>
> Carrying on down Larkhill Lane, there was McWilliams, another grocer's shop that my mother went in and then a haberdashery, followed by a newsagent's and tobacconist, and the barber's shop on the corner of Farrer Street. I went to Bob's the barber once a fortnight.

On the other side of Farrer Street was a butcher, a greengrocer, and on the corner of Townsend Lane was Lunt's, another grocer, which was handy if my mum wanted something quickly as it saved going down Larkhill Lane and I could go for her without crossing any roads, from quite a young age.

Everything seemed so convenient and with plenty of choice about where you shopped. Choice of grocer, sweet shop and greengrocer. Even the church we attended was just across the road. You could play in safety in the side street. The playing fields were only across the road in the other direction. The furthest places from home were school, the post office and the doctor, although there was a doctor nearer than the one we attended.

Doctor Campey was our doctor and he lived on the corner of Queen's Drive and Muirhead Avenue, where he had his surgery. There was no appointment system – just come along before closing time and wait. You had to remember who was in before you, so you would know when your turn arrived. The waiting room had a central table with magazines on it and dining chairs around the walls and on one side of the table. All was very hushed, so much that you could hear the clock in the house strike the Westminster chimes!

Liz Egerton remembers shopping in Litherland:

My mum shopped mainly at the local Co-op on Kirkstone Road and we knew the names of all the staff: Mona, Flo and Edna! Scott's Bakery had a red van that went around delivering bread and we would occasionally be allowed cakes. We ate good old-fashioned teas like corned beef hash and cottage pie and my mum always baked apple pies and bread-and-butter puddings on Sunday.

The rag and bone man would have balloons on sticks for us if we gave him old clothes. My best friend Lill's granddad owned the local piggery and we got to ride on his cart that Dolly the horse pulled along the roads, collecting the pigswill from each house.

Michael Moran, one of eight children, admires his parents for working hard to put food on the table:

My father worked on the docks, when he was lucky to be picked to work; he had to stand in a place called the pen and wait with hundreds of others for a ship to dock and be picked to help with the unloading. When Dad finished for the day, he would come home and look after us while Mum went out to clean offices at night to get the money to feed us.

I was on free dinners at school. I can remember the dinner ladies having two sets of tickets – one set had a number one on it and the other a nought. I got the one with the nought on it and was ridiculed by my class-mates because they called me the poor kid. I left school at fifteen to get a job – money was tight in our house and I left to help with the bills.

Christine McGarry had no affection for school dinners:

My mum didn't work until we were much older so she was always around. When at St Matthew's, I came home for dinner. I think most children did. However, when I made the transition to Bellerive, it was too far to come home. In fact, I made the journey on the 60 bus every day on my own from the age of eight – a journey of probably ten miles. I never felt frightened and never felt my parents worried about me. I had school dinners – greasy offerings and tapioca with a dollop of jam which had the consistency of wallpaper paste had to be eaten or we were in trouble. I eventually took a packed lunch – cheese butties, a chocolate biscuit and a piece of fruit. Mum never bought us crisps and we never had lemonade. It was water or tea.

Gordon Crompton did not stay for school lunch, but was busy elsewhere. He lived in Aigburth and, like many children of the 1950s, remembers shopping at the local Co-operative Store:

My mother drilled into us the Co-op or Coey number, which was 99821, when she sent us to the Co-op on Aigburth Road 'on a message' as she used to call it. I enjoyed going there enormously, especially with the overhead 'railway' system, when money was exchanged between customer and shop assistant and despatched to the cashier – Co-op employees did not deal directly with the customer with regards to cash. The negative side of shopping there was the way some adult customers used to treat us kids, telling us to wait our turn or get to the back of the queue, forgetting that most of the time we were there during our school dinner time from school.

Mary Allport remembers shopping for things other than food:

I used to walk with my brother to Marsh Lane in the cold to the gasworks to buy a bag of coke. It was shaped like eggs and we pushed the go-chair, now called buggies, there to buy a sack of these egglets. The men used to put the sack on our little go-chair and we would push it home.

Mary's first memory of shopping for clothes is: '… as a little girl, going with my mum, Aunt Mary and cousin Pat, who also lived in Queens Road, for new boots.'
Maddy Guest, born in 1944, has lived all her life in Bushey Road, Walton:

My auntie was a waitress and was always looking for black and white garments, so we used to go to Paddy's Market every Thursday and I hated it! My auntie used to buy me a toy to shut me up, then I would get dragged round. It was always packed with seamen with about six hats on their heads – the stall-holders called them two-shilling Johnnies. As I got older, I would stay home with Dad, and Mum would come in with a dress or a skirt for me and I would say 'Where did you get it?' and her reply would be 'Lewis's'. Otherwise I don't think I would have worn it!

Moira Kennedy remembers how her mother budgeted for new outfits: 'I had hand-me-downs from my sister, Anne, but also, my mum was in a clothes club in the next street, so we had new clothes paid for weekly.'
Eileen Pritchard also remembers new clothes and the excitement of treats:

I was bought two Sunday-best outfits a year at Easter and Christmas. I remember a green coat, in particular, and black patent leather shoes. I remember shopping with my mum and nan in the summer holidays and going, for a special treat, to the posh restaurant on the top floor of the Co-operative Store, Unity House, where I had my first Knickerbocker Glory ice-cream!

# 4

# PLAYING OUT!

In the 1950s, 'playing out' was an important part of most children's existence. Children knew their own territory intimately, just by spending so much time walking or running, hiding and making 'dens' in it. Even children who lived in houses with gardens 'played out', because that was where they met other children; most children in the 1950s knew and played with a lot of other children, beyond the small group of their special friends. There was also plenty of space to play and very little traffic.

Graeme Arnot, born in 1951, lived in Sherwyn Road, Anfield, in a house with a garden. He remembers street cricket:

When we were playing in the street with other children from our street and the neighbouring streets, we used to play cricket using the lamp post for the wicket. We often got told off by the neighbours for clambering in their gardens looking for the ball and were usually told to go down to the 'rec' to play.

The 'rec' was the large recreation ground on the corner of Townsend Lane and Richard Kelly Drive. Graeme continues:

Other games included football and kick the can, but we used a ball, instead of a can. Off-ground tick, ordinary tick, allalio, hide-and-seek, and skipping were played with the girls. One end of the rope, which was usually a long rope, was tied to the lamp post with a boy at the other end turning it. Six or eight boys and girls skipped and usually there was a chant that went with it. The girls used to tuck their skirts in their knickers so they wouldn't trip up. All the boys wore short trousers and invariably had scabs of some sort on their knees where they'd fallen over.

In the late fifties, I remember that, in winter, all the lads had duffle coats, black or navy-blue with hoods, or wore balaclavas, often knitted by their mums. Most lads had bikes and we used to ride around the streets in single-line formation. There wasn't much traffic on the roads in the 1950s, so cars didn't bother us very much.

In the summer months, we used to go on the 'rec' and meet up with other boys and girls, and usually had a game of football or sat around in the long grass. There were some of us that climbed on the railway embankment to see if they could see a train coming – and we would run like hell and hide when we saw a policeman.

There wasn't any fear then of danger from people who might harm us.

Joe Swindells lived in Knowsley, which was then a semi-rural area:

Living in the country, as I did, there were lots of places where we could make a rope swing. The bravest lad would climb high up in a tree and tie the rope to a branch. Then we would tie a broken branch to the bottom of the rope and sit on it to swing.

We would spend all day in the fields and woods, collecting conkers and bird-nesting – setting off with jam butties and a bottle full of water. On the odd occasion, we might have some lemonade powder to mix in it. Often we would come home with apples from local orchards tucked down our jumpers. There was also rhubarb to be had and peas from the fields.

We also played street games like kick the can, tick and hide-and-seek. We boys also played more daring games like split the kipper. In those days, it was quite acceptable for lads to have a sheath knife. Mostly we used them to form catapults from twigs or hack at branches in the woods to build camp fires. Split the kipper was where you faced your friend and each took a turn to throw the knife into the ground to the side of the other's feet and make your mate stretch his legs to where the knife was sticking. The loser was the one who could no longer stretch to the knife. Ollies, or marbles, was always a popular game and we would carry them around in a bag made from an old sock. If you had a 'steelie' – a large ball-bearing – you were on to a winner and much sought after!

Robin Bird remembers that, in Geraint Street:

There was a gas lamp outside with a rope attached for us to swing upon. I remember stroking the horse pulling the bin wagon, and the milkman with a motorcycle and sidecar rattling up the street. I remember there were different racial and religious groups living in the neighbourhood, but we did not mix. However, we often met children from these social groups in the corner shop when we went for Black Jacks with our sweet coupons. We mostly played in the street or entry and Mother took us to the park at weekends.

Barbara Doran, *née* Berry, lived in the Dingle:

I lived in a terraced house in Toxteth Grove, which is still there. I liked to swing on the lamp post at the bottom of the Grove. My sister broke her front teeth, swinging on a rope on this post. We played 'top and whip' and a lot of windows were broken with this game, and glass for windows cost half a crown, which was a lot of money in those days. We played two balls against the wall and tossing-up, where you ended upside down with your feet against the wall.

My mum worked as a cleaner in a big house, 11 Sunnyside, for the Smiths carpet family. Once, when Mum was sick, Miss Amy Smith came to see her. She arrived in her Rolls Royce and the chauffeur had to back the car down the Grove because it was very narrow for such a big car. What a palaver that was!

Anne Jones, *née* Yates, lived in Everton; she remembers lots of fun with her friends:

We played hide-and-seek, hopscotch, hoop and stick, blind man's buff, oranges and lemons, In and out those darkie bluebells, catch a girl, kiss a girl, truth or dare, the farmer's in his den and skipping games, like All in together and higher and higher, as well as tick, rounders, kick the can, paper chase, leap frog, knock and run, follow the leader, jacks and ollies, piggy in the middle and pudding or beef.

Anne Orme was born in 1946 and lived in Waterloo; she remembers playing hopscotch and many other games:

I can recall playing two balls on the backyard wall and then progressing to three balls; we would play for hours on end. Skipping was another pastime – we would have a very long rope and stretch it across Great George's Road and one girl would start skipping and then call the name of another girl to come and skip, and then the first one would skip out; this went on for hours too. Film Stars was another street game, where one child shouted the initials of a film star across the road. If any of the other children guessed correctly and shouted out the name first, they could take a step across the road until finally you all got across. The last child to get across the road had to call out the initials for the next game. It was fortunate that there was very little traffic!

Janet Arnot lived in Alderville Road, off Walton Hall Avenue. She recalls:

I often used to play hopscotch or skipping with other children in the street, with the rope tied on someone's gate, or in a small park at the top of our street where there were swings for babies and older children, a monkey ladder, two see-saws and a maypole. I often used to play on the swings after school waiting for my dad to come home from work. I remember swinging as high as I could to try to get my first glimpse as he came down the road from the bus stop. He always wore a trilby hat and a 'Humphrey Bogart' mac.

My sister, Pam, and I both had doll's prams and scooters. Pam's scooter was bigger than mine because she was older and it had a wooden footplate where mine was metal, painted red. Eventually, when we both outgrew our own scooters, I inherited hers but by then she didn't want to play those games any more. We weren't allowed to play out in the street on a Sunday. Outside the back door was a strip of concrete and in summer the rocking horse would be out there. We also had a tent which was put up on the grass to play in. I remember being given seeds to plant in the garden; they were night-scented stock, which my father liked because in the evening they gave off a strong scent.

David Russell also remembers waiting for his father to come home from work:

Townsend Lane, where I lived, had wide pavements and a central reservation where the trams ran, and, as a young child, I can remember waiting for my dad to come home from work and, as I waited, I would play trams by riding my trike between the lines of the pavement slabs.

One of my friends when I started school was Linda Jones; she lived opposite our house in the butcher's shop. Sometimes, when we were playing after school and the shop was closed, we played shop, but more exciting was when the binmen came and they took the bin out of the wall in the backyard. This meant that we could crawl through the hole left in the wall – I thought that this was good fun, but I'm not sure that Linda did!

I remember that, one winter, I got conjunctivitis from a snowball! I had gabardine, gloves, scarf and a woollen balaclava. The only bit of me that was showing was my eyes, so that's where the snowball landed!

Mrs Fisher was the caretaker of Clubmoor Presbyterian Church, on the corner of Townsend Lane and Cherry Lane, and my mum did the flowers on a Saturday for the Sunday Services. So on Saturday morning, June, Mrs Fisher's daughter, and I used to go with our mums, so that we could play in the church hall on our bikes.

I remember learning to ride a two-wheeler bike – my brother's – in the back entry, which was a wide one. I had to concentrate on the end wall of the entry which had a central pattern of bricks that had been re-mortared, but I really learnt with June on smaller two-wheelers on the local 'rec'.

In 1957, I got my own two-wheeler as a present for passing the scholarship and for Christmas. It was a Raleigh tourer with straight handle-bars. Apparently, it had been behind the sofa in the front 'parlour' for weeks before Christmas, but, as we rarely went in there, I did not know. About eighteen months later, I bought drop handle-bars. My brother's bike was drop handle-bars and both my friends, Dave Franks and Leigh Edwards, had 'drops'. Later, I changed the free-wheel to fixed, then I sprayed it pale-green and fitted gears. In order to do the frame, I hung it on the washing line in the back-yard and, using my mum's Electrolux vacuum cleaner with the special spray bottle filled with paint, sprayed the frame.

The mid-fifties was a time of 'playing out'; at first, this was only in the entry and in Huxley and Farrer Streets, but, later, once I had my own bike, it was farther afield. We would spend all day out playing and only come in for food. My friend, Dave Franks, had an older brother, Roy, who had a motorbike which, occasionally, we would have a ride on. Roy had also made a model motorboat and a model yacht. We would take these to the model boating lake in Newsham Park. One day he gave the motorboat with the engine to Dave and the yacht to me – I still have it today!

We used to play on the way home from primary school, 'ollies' or marbles, along Malleson Road. We played along the gutter; how we missed the grids, I don't know! We also used to play out after school on light summer nights and, at 5 p.m., we would all go to Mrs Fisher's house in Malleson Road to watch Children's Hour on BBC Television. There would be about six or seven of us. After Children's Hour, we would go home for tea. In Larkhill Lane, there was a building site. I don't know whether it was a bomb site, but they were building a small block of flats and we used to crawl under the gate and play in the new building as it developed – girls and boys!

Many children growing up in Liverpool in the 1950s made their playground out of the bomb sites left all over the city. The war was still a raw and painful memory for many adults and older children and this influenced younger children, even those who were not born until after the war was over.

Michael Moran remembers a war-scarred city centre and the debris remaining from the conflict:

I remember playing in bomb craters and the burnt-out shells of houses near the docks, close to my aunt's house on Scotland Road. We played cowboys and indians, influenced a lot by the cinema on Saturday. But we also played war, with the British soldiers killing the Germans.

One of the mad things I did was, after finding some fifty-calibre machine gun bullets, me and my friends lit a fire and played a game of chicken. We would throw a bullet into the flames and stand until one of us ran. He was the chicken. I realise now how dangerous it was, but it was a thrill at the time. I was never the chicken!

Mary Parkin also remembers the aftermath of the Blitz:

Next to our house was a piece of waste ground where the other houses had been, which we called the 'olla', probably a version of 'hollow'. It was full of bricks and rubbish and we would play there for hours. We also had air-raid shelters nearby, which were relics from the war and we often played in the 'airies'. I remember one game we played called 'Pork Shops'; we took enamel basins from home and dug around in the soil in the 'airy' and we found old bones and put them in the basins and pretended they were meat in the pork shop. I hope they were cat or dog bones, but the mind boggles if you think what they might have been!

Grahame Settle also has memories of the legacy of wartime:

The road I lived in was Hall Lane, a continuation of Long Lane where the Hartley's factory was, so I have clear recollections of the sweetish smell that permeated the neighbourhood when they were making jam. The factory chimney still bore its camouflage from the war, so was a notable local landmark. We had an air-raid shelter in our backyard, and a special treat for me was when the window cleaner came and would let me go up his ladder onto the top of the shelter.

Norma White, born in May 1945, recalls:

My childhood was spent in a house which had originally been a little general shop – the shop part was left as a time capsule – in Claudia Street, Walton, in the shadow of Everton Football Ground, where we children would mind bikes in our backyard for the men who attended the football match on Saturday afternoons; not many cars those days! I also spent part of every day of my early childhood at my great-aunt's house in Skirving Street, off Scotland Road and

Great Homer Street, as my mother used to go 'down home' every day to do their shopping. My great-aunt's house was totally demolished in the May Blitz and they moved into a house next door. As a child I used to play on the 'holla' with my bucket and spade, digging up pieces of broken pottery which I would take in to show my mother and she would say, 'Oh! that was a vase we had on the mantelpiece in the parlour' or 'It's part of a tea set my uncle had brought back from overseas.' The exercise stood me in good stead as I am still doing the same thing sixty years on, digging out the Williamson's Tunnels at Paddington where another chap and I are in charge of recording all the artefacts we dig up. Some kids never grow up!

Sometimes, to a child's imagination, the deserted ruined houses and spaces were not battle scars, but a magical landscape of infinite possibilities.

Pam Fitzgerald, *née* Prescot, describes this experience:

I well remember the summer of 1950 when I was eight years old, with my two sisters – Anthea, aged seven, and Pat, aged six – and three friends, Theresa Fenton and Wendy and Margaret Hilton. We played in the bomb site of the house next door to us. We lived in 'Newstead', a big, old house in Haigh Road, Waterloo. The house next door had been a very large semi-detached house, three storeys high with large gardens, front and back. We called it the 'Old Garden'. We had great fun those happy sun-filled days, making dens out of branches of trees – our wigwams – and lining them with long grass, leaves and bind-weed which grew profusely all around. I was always the Indian squaw and made little clay pots and bows and arrows out of the peeled branches of the numerous shrubs and trees for the Indian braves on their warpath. We dressed ourselves in bind-weed, willow-herb and evening primrose and made skirts of the grass and leaves; a pity we didn't own a camera then.

When we were inevitably bitten by midges or gnats, we used dock leaves to take the sting away. Mum would bring out our jam butties and lemonade-powder drinks for lunch – that to us was great fun. She had a bit of peace and quiet all day until she called us in for our evening dinner, after which, tired but happy children were soon asleep, dreaming of more adventures in the land of make-believe throughout that long hot summer.

Norma White, *née* Schafer, born in 1943, lived in Conyers Street, which ran from Netherfield Road to Scotland Road. She expresses a feeling that many children of the 1950s share:

Freedom was the best part of my childhood – we could roam around all day during the summer holidays, when the sun seemed to shine all the time.

A group of us would go to Stanley Park for the day, taking jam butties and a bottle of water and also a neighbour's baby in the pram; we would be there for hours with nothing untoward happening. I recall walking to the Pier Head, getting the ferry across and staying in the toilets and coming straight back, so that we did not have to pay.

We spent hours sitting at each other's front doors playing marbles or swapping comics, for those who were fortunate enough to have any. We did not have sweets and I cannot remember things like lemonade.

Christine McGarry remembers the freedom that children enjoyed:

I could go out all day long without any parental supervision and I travelled a fair distance, only coming home for lunch and sometimes not doing that if we'd got a picnic together. I use the word picnic loosely as it usually amounted to some jam butties and a bottle of homemade lemonade – made from either yellow or pink lemonade powder poured into the bottle of tap water. We would dip our fingers into the paper cone of powder so as not to waste the remains!

I spent a lot of time at 'the swings' just along the Drive, past Muirhead Avenue. There was a bowling green running parallel with Muirhead – it was always Muirhead or Townsend – the Avenue bit left off. But the bowling-green was alien territory and only for old people and, to be honest, we would have been given short shrift if we'd gone near! I spent my days at the park, which was next to the Mansion House, which housed the library. It was a large grey building with many fine features but how unappreciated by my philistine eyes. I was an avid reader – Enid Blyton had me enthralled – but next to the entrance to the Mansion House was a toilet, and I can still remember the pungent smell to this day.

The play area, where I spent many happy hours, was 'governed' by the Cocky Watchman who had a little hut in one corner, and woe betide anyone who misbehaved. I recall carefree, safe days swinging or hanging upside down from the monkey ladder or the hair-raising ride on the saddle, which was shaped a bit like a pirate boat. The 'jerkers' stood at either end and the crew sat along the length for what could sometimes be a frightening experience. Although I had plenty of friends living on the Drive, I was never bothered by going to 'the swings' on my own. There was one memorable day, when I was about seven or eight, and my mum had permed my hair; it may have been in readiness for my First Holy Communion. I had a head full of perm curlers, which needed to stay on for about twenty minutes or so, so I decided there was time to go to 'the swings' to fill the time. Needless to say, I had no sense of time and the end result was a distinct 'Curly Top' look.

Another site for play adventures was what we called 'Back Lane' which was accessed down Monash Road, and past a special school called Kilrea. This play area of swings and other play equipment fronted the railway line, which went past Broadway towards Orrell Park and to Halewood in the other direction. It is now a cycle path. I didn't care about any of those things then. We just had endless hours of fun clambering down the steep embankment and onto the lines – they were steam trains – I'm sure this activity was not allowed, but I don't recall a Cocky Watchman at this play area.

*From left to right: Christine McGarry with the 'Curly Top' look, friend, Olivia, and sister, Shelagh.*

More sedate times were spent at Larkhill Park which housed a beautiful lake and a particularly fancy, ornate bridge which we loved to stand on and feed the ducks. The grassed areas were sloped in sections and this was where we had our picnics.

We were so independent in those days but there wasn't the volume of traffic then. In fact, we were able to have a game of rounders on the Drive using the elm trees along the central reservation as two of the bases! I remember doing a traffic survey one rainy afternoon to register the different colours of cars, and it was a leisurely affair as you could sometimes wait maybe five minutes between vehicles passing!

June Buckley, living in Princess Drive, remembers the fun of playing out:

Going to Uncle Joe's Cabin on Mab Lane for Mojos, Black Jacks – four for a penny. Playing kick the can, chase the bunny and netball through the hoop of the lamp on the square near to our home. We used to play marbles on the grass near to our house, or two balls in the entry, or cricket and our next-door neighbour would always complain.

Mum used to give us some old clothes to take to the rag man and he would either give us a penny, or a small toy. We would also chase after the coal lorry and when the coal man shouted 'coal' we used to shout 'What do you feed your mother on?' and he would again shout 'coal'. We also used to sit by the kerb and take the numbers of cars and our Albert, my eldest brother, would tell us the make of the car.

Pauline Bennett recalls:

We were always playing out with friends: hopscotch, two balls, skipping, 'top and whip' when we coloured chalk circles onto the top and, in summer, bursting tar bubbles. Sometimes we dressed up and put on a show. We would go to the local chandler's with a jam jar for 'Aunt Sally' then, using a wire ring, we would blow bubbles.

Mary Parkin remembers many of the games that Pauline also played:

I played with two balls on the back door for hours on end; it must have driven my parents and grandparents mad, but there were all sorts of tricks you could learn to keep up with your friends. We also played with a long piece of washing line and played skipping games with various rhymes. If there weren't enough people to hold the rope, we would tie one end to the lamp post, but this didn't really work as well. I used to play for hours with my 'top and whip' and used stones that I found in the street to play Five Stones. We played hopscotch on the pavement using chalk to mark out the squares and we played marbles, but we called them 'ollies' and the big one, we called a 'bolly'. We played chasey and kick the can. If you wanted a rest from the game, you had to shout 'Barley – then you could join in again when you were ready.

There were many children's truce terms in use, including barley, fainites, scrips or squibs, pax and crosses, linked to the act of crossing fingers, which in some parts of the country performs the same function. Most of these words have their origins in the early languages used in these islands, including Old English, Old Norse, Old French, Anglo-Norman and, of course, pax is from the Latin for peace.

Bobbie Binks, living in Fazakerley, played out with his brothers:

We went every day after school to the local park, Hawksmoor Park, to play football and, quite often, Mum used to come down for us to come home, even in the dark. Happy days, I can tell you! On that park, they built a community centre and all the kids joined in to help. It was not a very big building; we called it 'the hut' and we were very proud of the fact that we were involved. The hut still stands proud today!

Chris Brocklehurst remembers:

… [the] big square at the back of the tenements in St Oswald's Street where all types of games were played – football, rounders and cricket. When we were a bit older, we would walk to all the local parks, among those we visited were Springfield, Sefton, Calderstones, Newsham and Edge Lane Botanic Gardens.

In 1833, a Government Select Committee on Public Walks emphasised the need for accessible space for public recreation to help improve the health of the urban population and to allow the social classes to mingle to some extent. Liverpool introduced a series of municipal parks, including those that Chris

Brocklehurst visited, and also the 200-acre Stanley Park and 130-acre Walton Hall Park. Some of these parks had been the grounds of large houses. There were also smaller parks that many children remember with affection, such as Larkhill Park and Greenbank Park.

Many of these parks had lakes for boating; some also had small ponds for model boats, where children spent many happy hours with a toy yacht or fishing with a net for tiddlers and 'Jack Sharps'. Some parks had bandstands, such as the one in Sefton Park, which is said to be the inspiration for The Beatles' Sergeant Pepper's Lonely Hearts Club Band. Others had glass-houses, cafeterias and open-air theatres, such as the one in Walton Hall Park, with afternoon concerts on Sundays and, in the summer holidays, concerts and talent competitions were held on other days too. There was a railed enclosure near the stage with deckchairs for hire, but there were always plenty of children and some adults watching from outside the railing. Most of these Victorian parks survive and still give pleasure to the people of Liverpool.

William Duvall also remembers the parks:

> Sefton Park played a big part in our childhood, especially in the holidays and weekends; also Princes Park – it was a good walk from our house, but there were no fat kids then. As I recall, the café in Sefton Park was very posh to us, but always busy.

Christine Deed remembers the local parks as part of her childhood, and also more local 'playing out':

> We often went to Walton Hall Park, or sometimes to Stanley Park, with either our own dog or other people's, and no money changed hands.
>
> My sister and I played out a lot; our house was on Walton Lane and our playground was in 'the Groves' off Luxmore Road – Nansen Grove and Golden Grove. They ended at the railway line so were quite safe from what little traffic there was at the time. We would be out from teatime to bedtime and Mum summoned us with an old iron hand-bell which she rang in the street. I think we were teased rather a lot about this but it was a fairly practical device.
>
> We had hide-and-seek games and running races. Great exercise, and I remember going home occasionally to get a drink of water and cool off. We also played hopscotch, Blind man's Buff and throwing tennis balls against the side wall of the corner houses in both Groves. The occupants were either deaf or very understanding because I don't think they complained. I spent many an hour trying to ride a bike, and I tried my sister's and a friend's roller skates with equal lack of success.

Gordon Crompton, and his brother and sisters, loved their shared bicycle:

> In early 1950, although we were poor, my mother was very resourceful and, by hook or by crook, managed to buy a bike between the four of us kids and this contraption was like gold dust to us all. However, not long after we got it, the elder of my two sisters was riding it in our street when an older lad came up to her in a threatening manner, demanding that she gave him a ride on it – obviously she had little option but to let him ride it or he would 'bash her lip'. So off he went towards the Dingle tenements. This happened late on a Saturday afternoon, so I wasn't home at the time because I had to deliver the papers on my paper round. As soon as my sister saw me, she told me what had happened, so I went straightaway towards the Dwellings, as we called them.
>
> My luck was in, because, as I entered the yard, which was like a huge playground surrounded by flats, I spotted a lad riding our bike. So without giving any thought to what might happen to me, I raced over to him and said, 'This is my bike – get off it!', which he did and away I went on it back home like a streak of lightning!

Gordon must have been a hero to his younger brother and sisters!

*Gordon Crompton, a heroic big brother!*

Anne McCormick, *née* Cullen, was born in September 1946. She remembers:

My parents were Annie and Billy and I started life in Walton living with my mum's family. We lived in three more houses with other friends and family, until in 1952 we got our own brand new council house 'out in the country' in Speke! I had a little sister, Maureen, by then. After the war years and living for the first six or so years of my life with other people, it was the equivalent of winning the lottery for my parents. They said they never wanted to move anywhere else or travel around after that. It is a rare thing nowadays to be content but they truly were content with their house in Speke for the rest of their lives.

Our playground was the woods and fields on the other side of the road from our house and, boy, did we make the most of it. We would make dens in the cornfield opposite until somebody spotted the farmer and we all used to leg it. We collected frogspawn in the ponds in the woods, picked bluebells and had picnics in the rolling meadows around us. On the way home from school we would climb one special tree in the woods.

My parents did not have spare money for toys so most of our entertainment involved outside games. I loved my 'top and whip' and we used to decorate the top with silver paper so it would make a lovely pattern when it spun around. I recall breaking the glass in the front door once when the whip got caught up in the top and flew from my hand smashing, into the door like a stone. I used to spend hours playing two balls up against the wall, tossing up against the wall and walking down the wall to make a crab.

When my cousins used to visit us 'in the country' they would annoy my dad by knocking on the front door and running round the side of our end of terrace to run in the back door. This was a novelty as they lived in rows of terraces where you had to go to the end of the street to walk up the entry to get in the back of the house. They would ask to have a bath in our house too, as they were used to going to the public baths.

As the oldest of the kids and the bossiest, I used to organise the games in the school holidays when my mum and dad were at work. Because at ten I had been a bridesmaid for my cousin, I had a white bridesmaid dress and so did my sister. So we regularly performed our own Panto in the backyard. Of course I was Cinderella because I had the dress and my sister would be the fairy godmother because of her dress. We would play music on the Dansette record player and all the other kids had a part to play. Sometimes we just had concerts.

There were lots of families and children in Speke and along our road in those days so we had lots of playmates. We would play rounders and cricket in the road using the lamp post for the wicket. We would go on the field opposite to play rounders and, if we were lucky, on nice evenings the dads would play with us while the mums had their chairs out on the front and enjoyed a good old natter.

Shirley Evans, living in July Road in a well-established community, remembers the same sort of neighbourliness that Anne remembers on a new housing estate:

We used to play out after school in the road and the neighbours would come out and watch us. They would sit on the low walls between the houses, watching us play rounders. If the weather was fine, some of the older neighbours would be wheeled out in their bath-chairs to watch us play. This was normal for us and we all felt very safe. Plus, there were few cars parked up or driving around then.

Unlike Shirley, Eileen Pritchard lived on a busy street in Kirkdale:

Our road was busy with traffic, so the children used to play in the back entry or a small cul-de-sac at the end of the street. I remember hiding from my parents when it was time to go to bed and being told off and kept in the next night. All the other children were allowed to stay out until very late – not me!

Mike Formby, born in 1945, lived in rural Lydiate:

I consider my childhood to be idyllic. We lived in a farmhouse; although my father was not a farmer, the adjoining land was farmed by my uncle and cousins and I and my young cousins and friends would 'help' when harvest time came. We would ride on the tractors, play on the bales of straw and stay out until the day's work was done. It always seemed to be warm and sunny – I can't remember many bad days.

There was a brook passing the farmhouse and this was a magnet for us. We would spend hours walking in the brook, seeing if there were any fish, and sailing, or trying to sail, homemade boats.

For a country child, visits to town were great excitements. Mike continues:

During the summer holidays when not 'helping' with the harvest, I used to go and stay with a great-uncle and aunt in Walton. There I got to play with children my own age and I remember going to Stanley Park with its lake and a lovely floral clock. We also went to Walton Hall Park and we took rides on trams to other parts of Liverpool; where we went I cannot remember but, as I'd never been on a tram before, it was very exciting!

I can also just remember going to Southport on the train from Lydiate station. I went with my grandmother – not the one who lived with us – and two cousins to the baths in Southport. My father was waiting to meet us when we arrived back at the station in the evening.

Lydiate station was on the Southport & Cheshire Lines Extension Railway which ran between Central station, Liverpool and Lord Street, Southport. It opened in 1884 and the line was designed to serve holidaymakers to Southport. Today, the line forms part of the Cheshire Lines Path, which is also part of the Trans-Pennine Trail cycleway and footpath between Southport and Hull.

# 5

# SCHOOLDAYS

Graeme Arnot started school in 1956; he comments: 'When I was five I started school in the infants. Mum took me on the first day but after that I had to find my own way there and back – a thing unheard-of in today's society.'

David Russell recalls:

I started school in 1950. My infant school was Roscoe Garsfield. On my first day, I came home and told my mum that my teacher was called 'Miss Turnip'. Her name was actually Miss Turner! My favourite teacher was Miss Schofield; she was young and fun! One day at school, I was told that I was 'Chinese' because I started my sums from the bottom of the page and worked my way up!

Infants wasn't bad because my brother was just across the yard and I walked to and from school with him until I was a bit older and had friends.

Junior School was Roscoe Ballantyne, which was up Larkhill Lane in Clubmoor. I can remember the bricks of this building looked like my favourite biscuits; you don't see them now but they were made of coconut and had a rough surface. This made me happy!

We had craft lessons – I made a face flannel with blanket stitching around the edge and another time my dad made me a loom from an old tomato box with nails along the narrow edges for the wool to go on. I wove the cloth and made a bag for my dad to put his shaving gear in.

*Roscoe Garsfield Infants, 1953: David Russell is second from left, second row. Friends, Dave Franks, second from right, back row; Leigh Edwards, extreme right, third row; and Brian Hudson fourth from left, second row. The teacher is Miss Schofield. It was Coronation year and many of the children wore red, white and blue rosettes.*

*Roscoe Ballantyne Junior School, 1956: David Russell is at the extreme right of the back row. Friends, Dave Franks is third, Dave Baddeley fifth, and Stuart Howard sixth, from right, on the third row. Brian Hudson is sitting on the front row, second from the left. The teacher is Miss Forbes.*

Mary Parkin had an early introduction to the world of education:

> My mum told me that I attended Prince Edwin Street Nursery School, though the only thing I can remember is the long walk we had and that we had a sleep part of the way through the session on green canvas camp beds. We were covered with grey scratchy blankets and, even if we didn't sleep, we were expected to lie still until the teacher told us to get up.

Mary stayed only two years at her first school and then moved on:

> I loved primary school and began at St Peter's, which was in Sackville Street, just behind our backyard. My first teacher was Miss Watson, who wore glasses and always had on a flowered overall buttoned down the front and lace-up shoes. I remember asking her constantly how old she was and her reply was always, 'As old as my tongue and a little bit older than my teeth!'
>
> Later, Mum sent me to Heyworth Street School, which was for girls only and was quite a walk away over Netherfield Road, which was quite busy. I remember Mrs McNeela, Mrs Priest, Miss Brandreth and Miss Barrowclough, who was the headteacher. Miss Jones taught us for the last two years of my primary education and used to read to us every afternoon, which I loved.
>
> Miss Jones taught us to sew and we had to cover the desk with a material cover to prevent the ink from the inkwells going onto our sewing. I was rather a large child and remember sewing a dress by hand when I was eleven years old – no mean feat for a child of that age but more so when you consider how big I was! We queued up to have Miss Jones inspect our hemming stitches, and we had to unpick any work that did not meet with her approval. I don't remember how long it took us to complete our dresses!

One of Robin Bird's main memories of his early schooldays concerns the weather:

> My sister, Erica, and I attended Notre Dame near the city centre and used to get the tram together to school. During the smogs, Mother wrapped a scarf around our mouths and made my sister and I hold hands during our unaccompanied journeys.

*Anne McCormick, in the middle row, fourth from right, at Stockton Wood Road School, Speke.*

Smog was caused by smoke from homes and factories; it was prevented from escaping into the atmosphere by thick fog. The portmanteau word 'smog' was used to describe the thick dark fog that reduced visibility so much that people could easily get lost in their own neighbourhoods. It was so dangerous to health, and the cause of so many accidents, that the first Clean Air Act was passed in 1956, although this did not immediately mean the end of smog.

John Halley, born in 1944, lived in Elton Avenue, Netherton, which was then a rural area:

My first school was an old army camp. What fun! The classrooms were wooden or Nissen huts, warm and cosy, with a coke stove in the middle, kept going by Mr Hudson, the caretaker. The boys loved playing soldiers, keeping watch in the old sentry box at the main gate. At Christmas, we wrote little notes to Father Christmas and the teacher would put them up the chimney of the coke stove. Sadly, we moved to a new school when I had been at school about two years and I did miss the old huts. Today, of course, these conditions would be seen as unsuitable, but we were happy and comfortable and receiving a first-class education. Our teachers were enthusiastic and lively.

June Buckley was one of ten children; she remembers:

We all went to Cantril Farm County Primary School, which is now Mab Lane County Primary. There was a lamplighter called Bill who used to walk with us to school every morning, and the school was a very tiny school surrounded by open fields, where the farmer had all his cows grazing. The farm was behind St Luke's Church in Princess Drive and we spent many nature walks in the woods, which are now Stockbridge Village and Brookside. We all went to Sunday School and took part in the Sunday School parades, led by the Boys' Brigade blowing trumpets and banging drums; we would go from the church along Princess Drive, around Mab Lane and back to the church, holding rope chains covered with flowers and wearing duster coats, white gloves, white sandals and pretty hats and dresses that my mum made. I can remember feeling so proud wearing our Sunday best. We only had a school uniform that we wore all week, having to change into an old dress, or shorts and t-shirt, and having just the one best outfit for a Sunday.

Our school had an anthem which was 'With My Hand on My Heart' and every Monday morning, a class would be responsible for taking part in Assembly. Every 10 January, it was the school's birthday and each class would send up a representative and be given a birthday cake, made by the school's cook, and a supply of books for their class. Miss Walsh was the headmistress and we had a ballet teacher called Miss Monkhouse and we used to put on some fantastic productions. One I can remember was *The Fire-Bird*, as I was the dragon's tail and my sister, Jeanette, was the dragon's head. I also remember the maypole and country dancing on a Friday afternoon.

Shirley Evans lived in Tuebrook:

My school was St John the Baptist which I attended until I was fourteen years old. We used to skip a lot at school, especially with long ropes, and it was quite a skill turning the ends. We all took turns turning the ropes and running in and out shouting and singing songs in time with the jumps and skips. Other favourites included two balls, played against a wall, hopscotch and 'top and whip'. We used to colour the top with different-coloured chalk dots. As it spun, these would merge to form a rainbow effect on the top.

One Christmas, the school held a Christmas show in Brockman Hall which was next to and part of St John the Baptist Church. I was one of eight fairies who had to do a dance and our mothers had to make our fairy dresses. This was different from the usual Nativity play with a choir that we used to do, but the shows were very popular and people looked forward to them every year.

Madeleine Roberts lived in Kirkby, still a rural area when she started school:

I went to school in Fazakerley, at Barlow's Lane School. My mum used to take me on the bus when I was in the infant school, but, when I was in the juniors, I went with my brother on the bus. I remember spending my bus fare on sweets and setting off to walk home, but my brother saw me and got off the bus and took me home on a later bus. Sometimes we could travel from Kirkby station to Fazakerley on the train. We used to sneak up the back steps in Kirkby so we had some money for the next day. My parents never found out, or there would have been trouble!

Barbara Doran went to St Paul's School in Byle Street from 1945 to 1951:

For being late for school dinner I was caned on the hand when I was ten years old, and smacked very hard on the legs when I was eight years old, for talking in class. I had red finger marks on my

*Dovedale Infants School: Ken Lloyd is sixth from left, back row. At this time, Jimmy Tarbuck and John Lennon were in the juniors, and George Harrison was also in the infants, but all of them were older than Ken and not in the photograph.*

*St Matthews RC Infant School, Queens Drive, c. 1953.*

legs when the teacher decided that I had been punished enough. I was always well behaved in her class after that and never late for dinner again!

The school nurse used to make regular visits to check for head lice and scabies. She gave out notes to inform your mum if you had either of these complaints. She used to tuck them in your socks to take home. Most children were given these notes at some time, which was quite embarrassing!

Margaret Dunford lived in Norris Green: 'I went to St Teresa's School and discipline was very strict; some of the teachers were nuns and they were very strict.'

Philip Baker, born in 1940, lived in Willow Hey, Maghull. Philip, who became a Professor of Linguistics, had an early, but initially painful, interest in language use:

School was St Andrews, Maghull. In my last year there, the slightly terrifying Miss Beck was one day trying to get us to pronounce 'castle' as 'carstle'. We resisted. At that time, my mother belonged to an amateur dramatics group and she occasionally got minor roles, usually as a maid. In the current production, she was supposed to speak with a Cockney accent and the local sweetshop owner's daughter happened to have married a Londoner. So she had helped my mother acquire some Cockney features for her role. This led me to tell Miss Beck that 'carstle' was Cockney and that I felt 'castle' was the correct pronunciation, particularly since there was no r in castle. This received enthusiastic support from most of the class and Miss Beck, to my surprise, immediately took me off to the headmaster, Mr Higham, after whom, at a safe distance, we were apt to chant 'I am the Great Higham, I am!' Higham sent Miss Beck back to her class, and then said to me that he agreed with me entirely about the pronunciation of 'castle' but would still have to cane me for challenging Miss Beck's authority!

Sue Jones was born in Eastbourne and came to live on Liverpool Road South, Maghull at four years old. She later moved to Coppull Road, Lydiate, where she was one of the first pupils in a new school:

I was about eight years old when I went to Lambshear Lane School and started there the day it opened. I remember Mr Pickup being the headmaster. Mrs Robinson taught the top class; everyone thought her to be very strict and we all dreaded going into her class but, in actual fact, once we got to know her she was really very fair; I think it was her broad Scots accent that frightened us.

Christine Deed went to Gwladys Street County Primary School from 1951 to 1957. She recalls:

School was just behind Everton Football Club's Goodison Park stadium and we stood in the playground in 1957 and watched the first tall floodlights being erected. It wasn't far from home and we walked along Walton Lane.

There was lots of drama, music and art. Also a musical play about gypsies for which we had to learn three songs, an annual puppet show, painting competitions (first prize 10s), a class play set in a courtroom, music on the wireless in the hall, a barn dance and a play for Liverpool's Charter Fortnight in June when everyone in the school was given a book called *The Story of Liverpool*, which I still have.

These books have been kept by many of the children who were attending Liverpool's schools in 1957 and have also been used by later generations doing projects in local history. They were an inspired gift by the Liverpool Education Committee of that time.

Chris Brocklehurst remembers:

I went to St Oswald's Roman Catholic School in Old Swan. While I was at school I got free dinners because of the size of the family. At school in the morning, we would get a small bottle of milk. The food we got in the school canteen had been cooked in a place in Green Lane and brought to the canteen to be reheated. I had no complaints about the food except for the sago, which was like frogspawn. When I was in the seniors, I was picked to be in the choir and also to be an altar boy.

Also when I was in senior school, we had two teachers who were Mr Fred Hall and Mr Lewis – I think they were ex-Army. Mr Hall would do gym work with us; our gym equipment was a box, a spring-board, two large coconut mats and a couple of medicine balls. Our gym was the school hall in St Oswald's Street by the church. Sometimes we would put on a display for the school and parents. The hall was used for everything – Cubs, Scouts, Brownies, Girl Guides, Catholic Mothers' Union and other groups.

Christine Deed remembers working hard at school:

In the final year, if not before, we had homework, probably in preparation for the 11+. I would have '50 sums and 50 English' for the weekend and there were regular maths and English tests. I was entered for the Margaret Bryce scholarship at Blackburne House and, in February 1957, I went there with Mum on the bus, taking 10d for school dinner.

This examination was for the Margaret Bryce Smith Scholarship. In 1908, James Smith, a Liverpool wine merchant, established a bursary for the benefit of Liverpool schoolchildren in memory of his mother, Margaret Bryce Smith.

In 1957, the scholarships were attached to the Liverpool Institute for Boys and Blackburne House for Girls, with the majority being awarded to boys. Some schools started coaching children from the age of seven, when they entered the junior department, for these bursaries.

Grahame Settle also took the Margaret Bryce Smith Scholarship exam. He passed it and then went to the Liverpool Institute:

I went to Rice Lane Junior School for Boys until 1953, when I progressed to the Liverpool Institute High School for Boys, thanks to a special scholarship. As a result of passing this, I didn't need to take the general scholarship exam. It was a Margaret Bryce Smith Scholarship, though it was always referred to as 'taking the Margaret Bryce', or 'winning the Margaret Bryce', without 'Smith'.

The exam was taken at the Institute, presided over by a master who became a deputy head, Mr Reece. On the day of the exam, we were given a special booklet to work through. Mr Reece gave us instructions, but he was quietly spoken and I missed most of them. Presumably they didn't affect the outcome to my disadvantage. Five scholarships were awarded that year, and that seemed about the norm.

In the top year at Rice Lane, our teacher was very keen on mental arithmetic, and tested us all every Friday morning. Getting less than 7 out of 10 meant a stroke of the cane on the hand.

At the Institute, the head wielded the cane to good effect, but class teachers favoured more individualistic approaches, such as throwing the board duster or using a gym pump.

I hated gym, being overweight and probably physically lazy. But I learnt to play chess, and that became my major hobby for many years.

Also, in about 1957, a friend taught me the rudiments of playing the ukulele. I graduated to the guitar, and that started another hobby. For three years, I was in the same class as Paul McCartney, but was never particularly friendly with him. Still, there was a general interest in pop music, as this was the time when rock 'n' roll was becoming known in Liverpool. My friend and I were great Buddy Holly fans, and attempted most of his songs; my friend was multi-talented as an instrumentalist. But we also liked trad jazz, especially Chris Barber, and it's sometimes forgotten that the Liverpool music scene in those days covered a wide range.

Eileen Kermode attended St Andrew's School, Maghull:

In February, I sat the 11+ exam and was very scared, but when I went into the room, the adjudicator was a Guider from Halsall whom I had seen at some Guiding events so I relaxed.

The headmaster had told Mum that he did not think I would pass – so we were pleased to prove him wrong! In September 1954, I became one of the founding pupils at Maghull Grammar School. This was not the best thing to be because there was no tradition to follow. Several children were brought from other schools to be the senior form. There were five teachers and the headmaster but throughout the first year there were additions.

Mary Parkin remembers preparations for the scholarship exam:

We were trained by doing exercises from First Aid in English and Alpha Beta Maths. I recently acquired a book with 11+ exercises and was amazed at the standard we achieved at age eleven.

Every week we had a mental arithmetic test and a spelling test and then the seating arrangements in the classroom were altered, so we all knew the pecking order and were aware of who was bright and who was not!

When I started at the grammar school, I was the only child in my neighbourhood to do so and hated wearing the awful navy-blue velour hat that First and Second Years at Queen Mary had to wear. I had quite a walk to the bus stop – at least fifteen minutes – then a fifteen-minute journey to the Crown public house at Stopgate Lane – then a ten minute walk to school. I was also the only child in my family to 'pass the scholarship'. I can well remember the ridicule I suffered on my way to school from other children, who called me 'College Pudding' – and wearing that awful hat didn't help!

Pauline Bennett recalls a big change in 1956:

> I went to Notre Dame Collegiate School in Everton Valley; we were actually measured for our uniform – it must have cost a fortune. My tunic was sponged and pressed each week and sent to the cleaner's at the end of term. It was a journey of two buses and I travelled by myself. None of my friends were going to that school, so it took me a while to make new friends.

Philip Baker reflects:

> One sad memory of the consequences of the 11+ was that I passed it and, because my brother was already at Merchant Taylor's in Crosby, I was given a place there free; in order to obtain some financial support from the government, the school had to accept 10 per cent of its students from those who had passed the 11+ and gave preference to those who had a brother there or whose father had been a pupil there a generation earlier. My best friend at the primary school at that time, who normally featured in the middle part of the class, was expected to pass. But he failed. He told me we could never be friends any more because I was going to a posh school. I told him that I wanted us to remain friends. A few days later, not having heard anything from him, I called at his house. He appeared at the door with his father. His father said that his son had to prepare for a lifetime of doing manual work like himself. My friend was crying. As he lived some distance from my house, I never saw him again. I am not saying that his father's attitude was common at that time. It is just an incident I remember with regret.

It is clear that the consequences of the 11+ were complex, and that some difficulties were experienced by those who did go on to a grammar school, as well as those who did not. It seems fair to say that the attitude of parents must have greatly influenced a child's confidence, self-image and adult life, regardless of the outcome of this exam.

Shirley Evans comments:

> I had been ill when we sat the 11+ exam; I managed to get a re-call at the age of thirteen years but I failed to pass. This didn't really have an influence on me, as I started work as soon as I turned fifteen for the Royal Liver Friendly Society in the Liver Buildings at the Pier Head.

Like Shirley, Harold Russell did not go to grammar school, but was later to enjoy a successful career; in Harold's case, in shipping. Coincidentally, he was to work in the Liver Building for many years:

> I left Roscoe Ballantyne and started senior school at Roscoe Garsfield Secondary Modern. I have many happy memories of my four years at Roscoe Garsfield. After getting over the idea of having individual schoolmasters for different subjects, and being introduced to a more strict discipline, I became involved in all the school's activities, particularly in the last two years.

Christine Deed started at the Queen Mary High School for Girls (QM) in September 1957. She remembers:

> We had a form committee which was led by a Form Captain and she had a badge. The house system was in force: Sandringham had a green badge, Clarence white, Buckingham blue, Windsor yellow and Marlborough was red. Inter-house competitions of all kinds flourished. We had house meetings at the end of each term, when there was great rivalry to gain the highest number of house points.

Christine also recalls school activities outside the classroom:

There was a school party in December on a Saturday afternoon with competitions, tea, dancing and games. We went to pantomime with the school in January, 1958, *Alice Through the Looking Glass* at the Playhouse. This was, I think, my first ever theatre visit. We were at the back of the balcony and the steeply raked seats made a big impression – I had a recurring dream of falling down into the stalls! I remember 'Children Singing' at the Liverpool Stadium in June 1959. We sang Humperdinck's *Hansel and Gretel*. I still sing in a choir.

Like Christine, Jean Cross, *née* Davies, attended QM. Jean remembers:

In 1951, the Music Advisor to Liverpool Education Committee, Bill Jenkins, together with Alderman David Lewis, set up the Merseyside Youth Orchestra (MYO). Young instrumentalists from all over the area were given the opportunity to have valuable orchestral training at the Philharmonic Hall. Meeting every Sunday morning, under the conductorship of Bill Jenkins, the orchestra went from strength to strength. Sir Simon Rattle began his career in the MYO as a percussion player, in the 1960s.

At QM there was a rich music tradition. Dr J.E. Wallace, who was also conductor of the Liverpool Philharmonic Choir, will be remembered for his outstanding musicianship and, together with Miss L. Norman and Miss J.B. McGibbon, directed many memorable Gilbert and Sullivan productions. 1958 saw the appointment of Miss Audrey Goodburn as head of music. Music was soon heard coming from every corner and cupboard of the school. The choir and orchestra grew in numbers and quality under Audrey's guidance and the annual inter-house music festival was always eagerly anticipated. The choir and orchestra performed regularly in school and in concerts for parents.

At that time, instrumental teaching in schools was very dependent on the skills of the music specialist and Audrey was also an excellent string teacher and instrumentalist. QM was also fortunate to have the artist, Olga Doran, on the staff, who also taught cello. There were no peripatetic instrumental teachers and if you had a yen to play a particular instrument that was not available to you at your school, then it was up to your parents to find and pay for private teaching.

Bill Jenkins set up many opportunities for young people to come together to make music. He assembled mass school choirs and recorder groups to give concerts across the city. My first experience of singing in a massed choir was at the Liverpool Stadium with the MYO. This was the occasion that triggered my desire to play in an orchestra. I also played in a recorder group at Liverpool Cathedral, a concert that was recorded by the BBC. I can still remember what we played to this day, O Beata Via, so strong and lasting was the experience.

I took up the viola soon after and joined the Liverpool Junior Orchestra together with three other classmates. This orchestra for younger children was also set up by Bill Jenkins as a feeder to the MYO. The orchestra met on Saturday mornings at Northway Junior School, Childwall, under the direction of Mr Michelle. I sang my first public solo at one of the concerts. I soon progressed to the MYO and also sang with the orchestra on many occasions.

As part of the ongoing training of young musicians, the Liverpool LEA set up a number of studentships, which enable gifted instrumentalists to have lessons with members of the Royal Liverpool Philharmonic Orchestra. A QM girl, Laura McKinnon, held one of these studentships and went on to become leader of the MYO. Under Audrey Goodburn's guidance, a continuing number of girls gained these coveted awards. In my class, four of us, all members of the MYO, formed 'The Queen Mary String Quartet': they were Dorothy Carter and Jeanne Watkiss – violins; Dorothy Lawson – cello; and myself – viola. We competed successfully in local music festivals.

*The Philharmonic Hall, famous for great music and the scene of many school speech days.*

Bill Jenkins' enthusiasm and encouragement across all Liverpool schools helped lead a massive musical surge in the city. Every youngster wanted to play an instrument. Liverpool's music, both classical and pop, was on the world stage. I was so fortunate to have been a part of this. I still play the viola in an orchestra, still sing as a soloist and direct musical productions for Operatic Societies.

Jean Cross has had an illustrious career in music; she is one of those who contributed to, as well as benefited from, the great and diverse musical culture of the city of Liverpool. From school, she went on to study the viola, singing, and piano at the Royal Manchester College of Music, now the Royal Northern College of Music and, later, taught music in secondary schools. She also taught violin in junior and secondary schools, and lectured on performing arts courses; she was a founder member of an operatic society and has been musical director of other operatic societies. She even performed leading roles in numerous operas and musicals. She has also performed as a solo mezzo-soprano.

As well as this, Jean has been a stage director for many plays and musicals, specialising in Gilbert and Sullivan. She played in the Chester Philharmonic Orchestra and has been principal viola. She has also written pantomimes, composed music for choirs and directed church choirs.

All this enjoyment of music, for Jean and others, grew from the opportunities available in Liverpool schools in the 1950s and '60s.

Janet Dalton went to a private school, yet never really enjoyed her time in education:

I went to Blairgowrie Prep School in Bootle from four to six years, then to Belvedere GPD School until I was eleven. The school was in Ullet Road and I travelled there and back by tram, unaccompanied, from the age of six. At age eleven, I moved to La Sagesse Convent School, Grassendale, which involved even further travelling from home in Walton. By this time, the transport was buses rather than tramcar.

I never liked school so left as soon as possible at fifteen and started work in Bibby's offices. I wanted to be a nursery nurse and so, at eighteen, I went to college in Manchester to train as one.

Dougie Cox passed the scholarship in 1951 and had similar feelings: 'I went to St Edward's College in Sandfield Park, West Derby. I can honestly say that I didn't enjoy it at all and was really glad to leave in 1956.'

Eileen Pritchard's arrival at school made a lasting impression on her:

My earliest memory was the day I started school at Arnot Street. I remember my father taking me and reporting to the office of the headmistress, Miss Wenlock. Then being taken to Mrs Jones's classroom; she wore a large wrap-around apron and looked like a granny; there was a large fireplace with a roaring fire and fireguard in front of it. I remember playing in a sandpit and painting lots of pictures. There was also a big bookstand with lots of books. We used to sit on the floor each day to have a story read to us.

I also recall going to one of the towers at the top of the building to take a hearing test – there were horrible stories about wizards living in the tower – scary! I remember the old smelly toilets at the other side of the playground – freezing in winter – and the fire drills and taking turns to ring the big hand-bell in my final year.

I remember the build-up to the 11+ examination and being told that the whole of my future depended on passing this examination. There was a lot of snobbery attached to which secondary school one went to. We had to go to Holly Lodge High School on Queens Drive to take the exam, which was nerve-racking in itself.

I was not academically brilliant – just a steady plodder and I did not pass outright; my parents were devastated. Fortunately, I had a recall, which took place at Queen Mary High School in Long Lane, Aintree – another journey to a strange part of Liverpool. Thankfully, I passed this test and was given a place at Evered High School. I was given a watch to celebrate my achievement.

My mother had to take a part-time job in order to buy my uniform and sports equipment. So from the age of eleven, I had to undertake jobs at home to help Mum – the weekly ironing, setting the table and washing up after tea, and cleaning my own bedroom. I continued doing the ironing until I married, aged twenty-three. If it was not done by the end of the week I was told I could not go out until it was done!

I also had to light the fire when I got home from school each night and I was often terrified when, after putting a newspaper against the shovel in front of the fire to 'draw' it, the newspaper caught fire and I had to get it onto the coals before it fell onto the rug.

I enjoyed Evered High School and took part in all the sports and drama events.

During the summer, the sliding doors of the classrooms around the quadrangle were opened and the smell of newly mown grass and the fabulous smell of strawberry jam from Hartley's Jam Factory drifted into the classroom. The scent of newly mown grass still transports me back to schooldays.

# 6

# SUNDAYS WERE DIFFERENT!

David Russell remembers:

Sunday was different. On Sunday we did not go to school or play out. We went to church and Sunday School. It really was school as we used to have an annual scripture exam. For someone who does not go overboard on exams – oh, what joy!

I went to Clubmoor Welsh Presbyterian Church on the corner of Cherry Lane; there was a Christian Endeavour group there, which was run by Margaret Morris. She must have run CE for fifteen to twenty years and seen many children. I joined as soon as you could which, I think, must have been eight or nine years old.

Christian Endeavour involved a form of church service with hymns and prayers, a Bible reading and a talk. The worst thing I remember was the 'chain prayer' which was meant to be spontaneous. I could never think of anything to say and always felt I must be the only person not to say an impromptu prayer. Overall, though, I think it was a good organisation. Our group was well run by Mrs Morris. We used to take the Morning Service in church once a year. This type of thing, plus the weekly meetings, gave us an opportunity to get up and talk in front of people and gain confidence for later life in doing the same thing in the workplace and elsewhere.

When my friends and I first joined we were not yet interested in 'girls' and were always thrilled when Mrs Morris said that we could play games in the big church hall after the meeting! Of course, as we grew older, CE was a good place to meet your friends during the week, boys and girls, as the education system at that time meant that we all went to different schools and wouldn't have seen each other otherwise. I went to St Margaret's Anfield (SMA) and other friends went to Alsop, the Collegiate or the Liverpool Institute. None of us went to a co-educational school.

The Christian Endeavour also ran holiday homes. David recalls:

I went with my mum and dad to Beechwood Court, which was within walking distance of Conway. I can remember that, at mealtimes, they beat a large gong, similar to the one shown at the beginning of Rank Organisation films. If you were late, you were expected to put some money in the charity box.

Bombardier Billie Wells, born in 1889, became British Boxing Heavyweight Champion and British Empire Heavyweight Champion in 1911. He was well known then for his prowess at boxing, but, later, was known better by succeeding generations as the 'Gongman'.

David continues:

It was expected that you would go to some form of religious service whilst you were staying at the CE holiday home, but no one forced you to go. However, as everyone was of a similar mind, people invariably put in an appearance at some time during the week as well as the Sunday service.

You had total freedom to come and go as you pleased, but there were organised activities for those who wanted them. These activities were organised by young students, who came as helpers for the summer.

*Clubmoor Welsh Presbyterian Church Christian Endeavour, 1958. (L–R) Back row: Margaret Morris, Malcolm Howard, John Evans, Revd William Morgan, Cynthia Walker, Betty Edwards, Laura Kirk. Middle row: Dave Baddeley, Dave Franks, June Fisher, Sylvia King, Elizabeth King, -?-, the McMurtry brothers, David Broster Front row: Leigh Edwards, -?- , Owen Fisher, Kenny Walker, Stuart Howard, David Russell, Brian Hudson.*

I remember being proud to be chosen as the captain of the cricket team and even more so when my team won! The teams were made up of all ages, as were the indoor games if it was raining. Again, I remember playing indoor cricket. This was made up of a matchbox for wickets, a small stick as bat and a table tennis ball. Runs were made by hitting the ball to the 'boundary', which was where the people were sitting to watch.

In the evenings, people did whatever they liked, but one night there was a concert organised by the entertainers, but largely made up of the holidaymakers reading poems or other 'party-pieces' or little acts that they got together to perform. I remember my mum read, 'The Soliloquy of a Safety Pin' and I remember my dad being a penguin in one of the sketches.

When we went, another year, to Kents Bank on Morecambe Bay, we went with my parents' friends, Mr and Mrs Evans and their son, John. I was older now and slept in a dormitory with John and two older boys. I remember falling out of bed one night.

Another day, we got up early and went swimming in Morecambe Bay, of all places. We didn't know then how dangerous it can be and we were up so early that there was no one about to warn us!

The early morning post train came through the little station at Kents Bank and collected the mail bags – I remember thinking that it was just like the post collection in my Hornby train set, where the bags were on a hook and the train collected them without stopping.

Later, as a teenager, I went back to Beechwood Court with my friend, Leigh Edwards. It was a good way to gain some independence by going on holiday without your parents but not without any supervision or organisation. There was a crowd of young people there, boys and girls, and we went about together and visited various beaches and places within reach, like Trearddur Bay on Anglesey.

Agnes Jones, *née* Webb, lived in Prince Albert Gardens, Park Lane. She remembers Great George Street Congregational Church:

*David Russell with his mother, Lilian, at Gwrych Castle, Abergele, while on holiday at Beechwood Court.*

Sunday School and church were very important to us. When we were younger, we had concerts and sang O, the Days of the Kerry Dancers, and I sang We'll Gather Lilacs and Waltz of my Heart. It must have been excruciating to listen to, but the worse our singing, the more everyone clapped! When we were a bit older we joined the choir.

My first holiday away from home was at a Christian Camp in Colwyn Bay. We were in a room with about ten bunks, all covered with patchwork quilts. There was a piano in the room and someone played and we danced. We'd walk through the woods down to the fun-fair and ride on the Dodgems. The boys would bump into us and try to make friends. The novelty of being away from home made it special.

Janice Pickthall remembers attending a church that has since been demolished:

I went to Sunday School at Breeze Hill Presbyterian Church, where I went to

*Dressed up for the Bethel Baptist Sunday School Anniversary: myself and Robert Radford; sisters Gwyneth and Barbara Jones (centre) went to Walton Church Sunday School. Most children went to Sunday School at that time.*

Christian Endeavour and also joined the Girls' Life Brigade (GLB). We had a Church Parade on the first Sunday of each month, when we would parade behind the Boys' Brigade and their band around Walton.

The Girls' Brigade, like the Boys' Brigade was founded to encourage young people to follow a Christian life. The motto of the Girls' Brigade is Seek, Serve and Follow Christ. Its aim has also been to offer fun and friendship to girls and young women.

Janet Dalton remembers the Guildry:

My sister and I went to Sunday School at St Nathanael's Church in Fazakerley Road, Walton and joined the Girl's Guildry there. As well as other activities, this involved marching round the roads following the Boys' Brigade band.

Some events marked off the seasons of the year – Easter, Whitsuntide, Christmas and Harvest Festival were all special occasions, and there were, for some children, the Sunday School Anniversary and the Sunday School Treat.

Sue Jones went to Maghull Methodist Sunday School:

I particularly remember getting prizes for regular attendance and for the Scripture Union Exam. Then there were the Sunday School Treats – usually to Botanic Gardens, Churchtown or Otterspool. We would travel by double-decker bus and there was always a scramble to get upstairs. Once at our destination, we would enjoy games like rounders and hide-and-seek and then there would be races, three-legged, egg and spoon, sack races, all great fun! Finally, we would settle down for a tea of sandwiches, fairy cakes and lemonade before making our way home, exhausted but happy.

September would be Harvest Festival when we all took fruit and vegetables to decorate the church. Then, of course, Christmas would mean a party in the church hall and a visit to The Royal Court, Empire or Playhouse to see the pantomime. The church was quite a focal point of our lives.

Grahame Settle also recalls Sunday School outings:

My elder brother and sister were very involved with Warbreck Moor Methodist Church, so I went to Sunday School there. Outings were to Helsby Hill, and featured games, sandwiches and general mayhem. Of course, it never rained – in my memory, anyway. I can't remember much about the Sunday School organisation. I know that I enjoyed going. At ten or eleven, we were invited to start attending part of the morning service; then the youngsters like us would be taken out before the sermon to rejoin the Sunday School. Unluckily, the first time that a friend and I went along, the group we were meant to sit with had been displaced by a Baptism party. We inadvertently sat with them instead, and I found it all acutely embarrassing and didn't go again. My friend was obviously made of sterner stuff, as he carried on attending.

Janet Arnot enjoyed the Sunday School Treat:

I went to St Aidan's Sunday School in Cherry Lane. We met at church for the Treat outing and travelled on a hired bus – I can't remember where we went, but I do remember that we all looked forward to the treat and had fun. There were races, such as egg and spoon, and bean bag races and a picnic lunch.

I also remember collecting the pretty little text cards that were given out each week by the Sunday School teacher.

Text cards were small cards, sometimes no larger than an inch square, usually with a picture of flowers, animals or a country scene printed on them and a text from the Bible. They were often given out by Sunday School teachers. In earlier times, the children were expected to learn the text and be able to repeat it on the following Sunday, but, by the 1950s, they were usually just an added attraction for Sunday School attendance. Although some featured ships and planes, they were especially popular with little girls, including Gill Shaw.

Gill Shaw's first Sunday School was in Quorn Street. Gill lived in Canova Street with her parents, Fred and Joan, and older brother and sister, Fred and Shirley:

> We went to York on an outing. I suffered from travel sickness all the way there and back. One of the male teachers sat with me to try and take my mind off it. He never complained, although I'm sure I ruined his trip. I can never go to York without remembering his kindness.
>
> Later we went to Sunday School in Kensington. My brother or sister would take me as Mum said I was too young to cross busy roads. There were little chairs all painted different colours, red, yellow, blue and green. The teacher was lovely; she had teenage girls to help her and I won a colouring competition and got a book for a present. I loved going to Sunday School – it was so nurturing – I loved hearing about Jesus. My granddad gave me my Bible; it's black leather with a zip all round it, complete with pictures. I loved the little cards we were given by the teachers. I also remember Whit Sunday in our pretty dresses, white ankle socks and ribbons in our hair!

*The Mersey Tunnel: Eileen was not the only child who wondered how safe it was!*

Eileen Pritchard also remembers the Sunday School Treat:

> The first time I travelled through the Mersey Tunnel was on the Sunday School Treat to West Kirby on a double-decker bus. I was terrified that the tunnel would collapse and we would be drowned. Church played a big part in my youth – Sunday School, then church at night; Brownies and Guides; youth club; being part of the drama group and putting on plays.

Mary Parkin also became involved in the life of her church:

> I attended Sunday School at St Ambrose Church, which was twinned with St Timothy's, and I took part in various activities and pageants they organised. I eventually became a Sunday School teacher. I visited the vicarage in Shaw Street with other girls for tea and can remember how 'posh' the vicar, Mr Hill, and his wife seemed to be. On reflection, they probably were quite well-to-do and came from privileged backgrounds. Mr Hill was called James

Carthew Hill, and wore a signet ring on his little finger, which was really unusual. I thought Mrs Hill, whose name was Muriel Beatrice, was wonderful; she wore tweed suits and lace-up shoes and a floppy felt hat. I think she was much younger than she looked!

Hazel Rimmer remembers dressing for a special occasion:

I attended County Road Methodist Church and Sunday School. For the Anniversary, most children had a new outfit and you had to attend morning, afternoon and evening services. Sunday School outings were usually to Woolton Woods or Helsby. We all looked forward to travelling through the Mersey Tunnel, which was a rare occasion.

Ann Cowley comments:

I remember that being a Catholic was hard work when I was young. We had to fast for twenty-four hours – no water even – before we could have Holy Communion. When I was eight years old, our teacher was called Miss Cunningham. We had to know our Catechism off by heart; if we didn't she would call us out and smack our hands with this rubber strap. It was so painful. My opinion now is that she must have been a sadist. She would twist her mouth up in this horrible contorted way as she proceeded to smack our hands.

The fear we felt going into school on Monday morning, if we hadn't been to church on the Sunday! Father O'Shea would ask if we had all been to Mass the day before. Those of us too scared to admit we hadn't, would be asking the other kids who went to Mass, what colour vestments he had on, just in case we were caught out.

In senior school our headmistress was a nun, called Sister Veronica. She was over 6ft tall; looking back, she could easily have been a man in drag. She would cane us if we were naughty in some way.

I lived with my grandmother; I called her Nin, and my Auntie Mary and Uncle Gilbert, Gilly for short. Every Sunday Nin and Mary would prepare the roast dinner. My Nin would be chopping the carrots and turnip up, singing really fervently, a hymn, 'Faith of our Fathers'. Auntie Mary would be singing ever so gently 'Our Mary we Crown Thee'. They were so funny.

Maddy Guest remembers preparing for her First Communion:

We had to do a practice run for Confession. The teacher sat one side of the big free-standing blackboard and you sat on the other. I was mortified as I had to tell that I'd helped myself to raspberries from a bush in the allotments behind our house. I never thought of just saving it up for the priest!

Pat Gilbert, one of seven children, looks back: 'I can remember making my First Holy Communion and Mum couldn't afford to buy me a new dress. An old aunt got me one from the market for 5s and I had a little posy of forget-me-nots!'

Susan Williams, *née* Kehlenbeck, born in 1947, had an idyllic childhood in Little Crosby:

At seven, I made my First Holy Communion early on Maundy Thursday morning. After, we had breakfast at school and our photograph was taken in the priest's garden. As a treat, we were allowed to visit the chapel in the Convent.

Church was at the centre of our community in Little Crosby. The parish priest, Father Laurence Anderton, was a lovely man; he always had time for a chat. The year was punctuated with church processions honouring Our Lady or the Sacred Heart and there was Harvest Thanksgiving. At Christmastime, the children went to Crosby Hall to sing carols for the squire, his wife and family.

The event was held in the library – I was fascinated by the book-lined door. We were given biscuits and hot orange juice. The grounds of Crosby Hall were the venue for school Sports Day, which I always enjoyed. It was followed by tea outdoors and I can't remember it ever raining!

Jim Greer remembers:

Our mother, Hannah, used to ask the cobbler in Byrom Street to put iron studs in our clogs to make them last longer and, when we went to church on Sunday, everyone would look round when we walked down the aisle.

But Jim points out that many of the important lessons about honesty and right and wrong were also taught at home:

I was sent to the local baker's one day for some bread and found a 10s note on the floor, which I took home to my mother, who, despite not having much money, told me to take it back and give it to the baker. If we were playing out and broke someone's windowpane, we were taught to knock on their door and offer to put it right. These were the values instilled in us – respect and honesty. People like my mother were the backbone of this country!

Barbara Doran was a member of the Salvation Army Dingle Corps, based in Park Road near to the Overhead Railway station:

There was something to do every night of the week, from singing, to band practice, to youth club. The Salvation Army Rose Queen festivals were something to behold. The festival was held yearly in June. We would parade around the streets dressed up in fancy-dress costumes and then go back to the Army hall, where the Rose Queen would be crowned.

One year, I remember my sister covered my arms and legs with gravy browning and I was a hula girl in a grass skirt. The only trouble was that it started raining and I had brown and white striped legs when we got back to the hall. How awful I felt!

I also remember when the Salvation Army was visited by Catherine Bramwell-Booth. She arrived in a carriage pulled by horses and she gave me and my sister a ride in the open carriage. It was so exciting! But my mum was not pleased because I had on a dress that was all torn and my sister was not too smart either. My mum said that we had been paraded around the streets of Dingle looking like scruffs.

*Pat Gilbert's little sister, Maureen, after her First Communion, with their eldest brother, Robert.*

Catherine Bramwell-Booth CBE (1883–1987) was a Commissioner in the Salvation Army and granddaughter of the Salvation Army's founder, General William Booth. She dedicated her life to the service and ideals of the Salvation Army. The Salvation Army, founded in 1865, is an evangelical Christian movement, with a worldwide and highly respected commitment to charity and social service.

For Maurice Levene, it was Friday evenings and Saturdays that were different from other days. Maurice Levene and his parents, Doris and Isidore, attended Princes Road Synagogue, where his parents had married:

> I always loved music and was in the choir from age ten to eighteen and trained as a Cantor for four years and passed the exam. I helped at Greenbank for ten years and also Princes Road. I did not come from a strict Orthodox family, but we always had the Friday night meal with the family, when the Sabbath begins just after sunset, and we attended the Saturday afternoon service. I remember my Bar Mitzvah. It was held on the Sabbath with a celebratory lunch afterwards.

Gordon Crompton was a chorister and remembers conflicting options for his spare time:

> I joined the 46th Liverpool Company of the Boys' Brigade and stayed until I left at sixteen years of age – my mother insisted that I be in the choir of St Michael's in the Hamlet, go to choir practice on BB band practice nights and be in the choir on Sunday mornings and evenings. I must admit I was not very ambitious as I left the Brigade the same rank as when I joined. I only wanted to play the drum in the band, play football and go to camp, as I found the regimental routine very boring.

The Boys' Brigade is a Christian youth movement founded for boys in Scotland in 1883 by Sir William Alexander Smith. Its motto is 'Sure and Steadfast'; the movement aims to promote self-respect, self-discipline and Christian values in boys.
Gordon continues:

> Whilst in the choir, I did sing solos during anthems, but I didn't particularly like the choir until I acquired a mouse called – surprise, surprise! – Mickey. I used to take him to choir practice and Sunday services and caused great amusement amongst the other choir boys.
>
> I loved playing snooker and table tennis and I was in a club called St Michael's Church Club, situated in St Michael's Road. Before I attended, there used to be Bible Classes there, but later the church just paid the rent. The caretaker of the club used to allow me and my mates to play snooker there on a Sunday morning, but first, we had to clean all the downstairs rooms and collect the coal from the cellar – I loved the place!

It is clear that in the 1950s, as well as receiving a good grounding in morals and values, the various denominations were also offering activities and opportunities to young people to have fun; and, as they grew up, to meet the opposite sex in a safe and supervised environment. Very few young people were allowed to wander the streets in the evening and parents, in general, wanted to know where children and teenagers were going, and with whom, before they were allowed to go out.

# 7

# GOING ON HOLIDAY

For some children, peace brought immediate and dramatic changes. Harold Russell was seven in June 1945:

> My first big holiday with Mum and Dad was in the summer of 1945. We flew to the Isle of Man in a silver bi-plane and our luggage was in a camouflaged bi-plane. I can remember that the lifebelts under the seats were the round type that you see on a ship or by a pool.

Pauline Bennett remembers many happy childhood holidays, as early as 1951, when she was seven years old:

> We went to Butlin's at Pwllheli for a week's holiday and I remember my first taste of Coca Cola. Another time, we had a fortnight's holiday in a lovely bungalow in Dyserth, North Wales, with another family – friends of Mum and Dad. The bungalow was what we would now call a boarding house. It had a lovely garden, and I collected snails in a jam jar.
>
> In 1954, Mum and Dad bought a four-berth caravan and put it on a farm at Cwm, near Dyserth. Dad installed running water – cold, of course – but the toilet needed to be emptied regularly! The caravan was put on a concrete base in a field. These concrete bases had been put there during the war; I can't remember what for, but it was something to do with the army. The farmhouse didn't have any electricity, they burnt oil lamps. We could take friends with us to the caravan; we slept 'top and tail' in the side bunks, double bed or on a foam mattress on the floor. Mum and Dad slept in the van. There was limited storage space and no fridge.
>
> We helped the farmer, milking, getting the hay in, rounding up sheep, cutting thistles. My brother and I preferred to stay and help on the farm to going into Rhyl or Prestatyn with Mum, Dad and my younger sisters. By the mid-fifties, I was steering the tractor round the fields to the hay bales, where the farmer and his son loaded them onto the trailer. We would then help to get them stacked in the Dutch barn back at the farm. I learnt to drive a van in the field, steering between straw bales and progressing to taking water in churns to the animals in the fields. During school holidays, we stayed weekdays by ourselves; Mum and Dad sometimes came out mid-week, but mostly on Friday night. We didn't have any fears. For city dwellers, we have very fond memories of life in the country.

Graeme Arnot remembers that:

> … holidays in the early 1950s tended to be a make-do affair. We used to go to a caravan or Mum and Dad hired a cottage in North Wales. They were happy occasions but I only have fleeting memories of them. Dad had a motorcycle and sidecar combination until 1954 when he bought his first car, a four-door black Austin; when we went out, my brother and I and my mother and father used to look out for other cars that were the same and the first to spot one would cry out 'There's one like ours, four-door black!'
>
> In 1959, Mum and Dad bought a small chalet near Llangollen from my uncle and we went every weekend during the summer months. Dad finished work on Saturday morning around about one and when he got home had a small lunch, then we packed up the car and off we went

through the tunnel to Wales. I was always very excited and usually sick by the time we reached Birkenhead. I was usually sick two or three times more until we got there. Strange it was, but I was never sick coming home on Sunday afternoon.

When we were at the chalet I met up with other boys who had chalets in the area and we roamed around the mountain all day without any fear either of getting lost or any danger that might be around. We picked whinberries and blackberries. There was also a gate across a mountain road that people used to have to get out of their cars to open, before they could go along the mountain road. It was a favourite task of a couple of us to wait by this gate so that we could open it for the motorists and, at the same time, hold our hand out for the tip that we hoped to get. This could prove to be very lucrative on a Sunday. Unfortunately, it wasn't long before they put a cattle grid in instead of the gate and the venture stopped.

Terry Arnot, Graeme's elder brother, also remembers family holidays, some of them before Graeme was born:

During the late forties and early fifties, my mother and father and I would go for a week's holiday to Rhyl, on the North Wales coast. We travelled by Crosville service bus, which ran from outside the Birkenhead Ferry Boat station and reached Rhyl via Prestatyn. Our accommodation was in a traditional boarding house run by, would you believe it, a Mrs Jones, who provided breakfast and an evening meal.

As a nine or ten year old, I thought Rhyl was the most wonderful place on earth. Every morning was spent on the beach or the promenade. I particularly remember the boating lake with the small hand-driven paddle boats; also the two-wheeled bicycles, which could be hired and ridden round a rather small concrete circuit. Afternoons were usually spent taking bus rides to local places of interest, particularly the castles at Rhuddlan, Conway, Caernarvon and Denbigh, or the other coastal resorts, Llandudno and Colwyn Bay.

My father knew North Wales very well. Before the war, he had been a lorry driver for a road haulage firm, delivering to all the towns and villages between Liverpool and Aberystwyth. After the war, he progressed to become transport manager of the company, F.D. Hulse Ltd, which was based in Parliament Street. When the Attlee government nationalised road transport, the company was absorbed into what became British Road Services (BRS); he then became superintendent of the BRS Depot in Lightbody Street, which again specialised in deliveries into North Wales. In 1951, the Churchill government de-nationalised road transport and F.D. Hulse was recreated in the private sector. Their new depot was in Grafton Street, where my father resumed his position as transport manager. I don't know how he regarded the political aspects of nationalised road transport, but I do remember him saying that the BRS 'had too many bosses'.

*Myself with my father, Alf, and little sister, Janet, on a caravan holiday at Tyn y Morfa, on the North Wales coast.*

North Wales was a popular holiday destination for many Merseysiders.

William Duvall remembers:

We just had great times every year. Talacre, like it is now, was a main holiday spot for most Scousers in the fifties before package holidays. Mainly prefab-type chalets, some brick-built, but not many. My parents rented one from the woman who owned the corner shop; her name was Maisie Catterall. Back then, Talacre consisted of a general store-cum-café owned by people named Taylor. They had two places, the other being an arcade with the usual slot machines and ice-cream bar. The store was the main attraction for us because it had a Wurlitzer jukebox. We listened to Radio Luxembourg when we could, but the jukebox was very American and was always up-to-date. The Shadows, The Beachboys, Buddy Holly, Elvis – all before the mop-tops took over and the music really took off. At threepence for one play or 1s for five, we always made it our first stop when we finally arrived.

We travelled there in a Morris Minor van-type of car provided by the tally man. There was probably a charge for this, but we children did not understand such things. My stepmother made a deal with the tally man – how much I do not know, but I believe it was common practice for most people in those days. There were at least six of us in the back of a Morris Traveller. It was a dreadful journey.

We spent all day on the beach; it was much bigger then – huge dunes and marram grass. There was a place we called the hidden valley; it was full of old buses and furniture vans converted for living in. How old it was I do not know, but my dad said it had been there for years. There were a bakery and dad would drag us there for bread and pies and Full Swing lemonade. There was two clubs in Talacre; one for the peasants like us and one for the posh bods. Dad and Mum spent a lot of time in the club before games of cricket or swimming – the water was clean then or maybe we were not too fussy – then pilchard butties for dinner. Dad often walked us boys up to a place called Gwespyr through the woods. There was always a pub at the end of the walk and a bottle of pop and a bag of Smith's crisps before the trek back in time for tea. My stepmother always bought a food hamper to take with us, full of Tyne Brand tinned meats. I think she bought it from the catalogue; anyway, we always ate well on holiday. Despite our hard upbringing, we had a lot of good times and good holidays. I have taken my own children and grandchildren there many times and still go for the odd day with my wife, Val. Although it has changed a lot – it's more up-to-date – it is still more or less the same.

Christine McGarry also holidayed in North Wales:

We stayed mainly in Prestatyn. We had a week every year and went back to the same house where Mrs Bennett, for the sum of £5 per week, bought food and cooked for the four of us. We spent our days on the beach making sandcastles and we were allowed a daily donkey ride and pennies for the slot machines. We made our way to Prestatyn on public transport as my father did not purchase his first car until I was sixteen.

Liz Egerton remembers happy times in Gronant:

We holidayed in Gronant, in North Wales, on a site that was known as The Warren. There were loads of higgledy-piggledy bungalows and caravans. The first time we went we stayed in a disused railway carriage with a stove in the middle! Fantastic memories! We played the card games Donkey and Happy Families to amuse ourselves.

Linda Leaworthy stayed at the Robin Hood Camp in Rhyl: 'I can remember going there when I was about three. Our chalet was right next to the railway track and it used to shake when the trains went past!'

Joan Munro, *née* Lee, born in 1947, remembers Pwllheli:

Our holidays were usually spent at Butlin's holiday camp in Wales. It was pretty sparse in those days, with toilet blocks and hot water to wash brought round, but we enjoyed ourselves and it was the highlight of our year.

Eileen Pritchard also enjoyed early family holidays at Pwllheli, but soon became more adventurous:

My dad saved all year to take us on one week's holiday to Butlin's Holiday Camp in Pwllheli. We went every year until I began going away with the youth club or school when I was about fourteen. The journey took all day on a coach to get there; it now takes a couple of hours. Dad's second week's holiday was spent on days out to New Brighton, Southport or Blackpool. We did not have a car so travelled most of the day to get somewhere for a couple of hours before returning home.

I was very fortunate to go on holiday to Larne in Northern Ireland nearly every summer, as my nana's sister lived in a bungalow on the coast road. Looking out from my bedroom window, I could see the Stranraer ferry coming and going each day from Scotland. I loved these holidays as I think Ireland is a wonderful country with magnificent scenery. I think my friends back home thought we were very rich because we travelled so far – some of them did not have holidays.

We travelled by ferry from the Pier Head to Belfast on what I would describe as cattle boats, as cattle were transported on one of the decks. The crossings were very rough and on one trip my mother was in the toilets all night being ill. I was terrified to move to find her in case I got lost – I was about ten years old.

When I was twelve, I flew for the first time from Liverpool Airport to Belfast. I actually flew on my own to join my nana! My dad was able to take me to the foot of the steps on the plane and hand me over to the stewardess. On arrival in Belfast I was met by my nana and uncles in their car. I felt very important and quite brave.

When I was at Evered High School, a trip to Sitges in Spain was arranged. I was fifteen and desperate to go, so I found a Saturday job in Littlewoods shop on Walton Vale in order to help to pay for the trip. My friend, Pam, was put on the lingerie counter – I was assigned to the bacon, cooked meats and cheese counter – ugh! I hated opening the cheeses, particularly the blue cheese; my clothes smelt of bacon and cheese and I could not wait to get home and wash my hair. I had to strip down the large bacon slicer at the end of the day and wash it thoroughly – it was very hard work.

I earned enough to help my parents pay for the Spanish holiday. We left Lime Street station at midnight on a Thursday and travelled to London, then changed trains to get to Folkestone, then onto the ferry to Boulogne. A further train to Paris, where we boarded yet another train for a fourteen-hour journey to Spain. We arrived at our pension on the Saturday evening. I took one look at the food and decided that I was not going to be able to eat anything and, consequently, would die of starvation. However, after a good night's sleep, I was ravenous and ate everything put in front of me. We had a great holiday visiting Barcelona and a bull fight – ugh! – and a monastery. Then we had the horrendous journey back home.

I loved the apricot jam made in Spain and decided to take two jars home for Mum. Not a good idea; when we opened my case, they had smashed and Mum had a terrible time getting the glass and jam out of my clothes!

Eileen's account of her first aversion to exotic food, then her realisation that it was enjoyable and, finally, her wish to take something home to share with her parents, even though it was an unsuccessful attempt, is very much in accord with the spirit of the times. Foreign travel was introducing people of all ages to food items and recipes that were new to them and which they enjoyed and wanted to eat at home. The 1950s was a decade that saw the transition from the rationing of even basic items to the beginning of a revolution in the nation's eating habits.

Sue Jones also remembers holidays spent staying with other members of her family:

> My maternal grandparents and aunt played a bigger part in my childhood than my father's family because we lived close to them. I do, however, remember that every summer we would go to Eastbourne for a fortnight's holiday – staying with my grandmother and visiting my aunts, uncles and cousins. We would travel by coach from Edge Lane to London Victoria where we would change for the bus to Eastbourne – the journey from Liverpool was overnight and so was quite exciting. The sun always seemed to shine while we were on holiday and we spent most of our time on the beach – I remember that we used to go to the Eldorado beach café and get a pot of tea and all the cups, saucers, etc. and take it onto the beach where we would have our picnic. We would pay a deposit for the crockery – no throw-away cups in those days.

Dougie Cox remembers holidays with his family: 'We spent summer holidays in Moreton, camping on the big field in our tent and cockling. Later on it was off to North Wales for a holiday in a caravan.'

Shirley Evans remembers many enjoyable holidays:

> We went on a holiday every year, travelling by train, as Dad worked for the railway and was allowed five free journeys a year. We would stay in a farmhouse in Ruabon, near Wrexham, in North Wales. I remember having to leave a clean plate every mealtime. We also had holidays in the Isle of Man, which we would travel to by boat from the Pier Head. My favourite picnic memories are from Laxey Beach with jam butties and cold tea from a lemonade bottle.

Janet Dalton, whose father was a cow-keeper who ran a dairy in Walton, remembers the disadvantage of a family-run business:

> The downside of my dad being in the milk business was that we could never go away on holiday as a whole family, as either Mum or Dad had to be there 365 days a year. But my mother took us on a summer holiday each year to Llandudno, the Isle of Man, or Bournemouth, staying in boarding houses serving breakfast, lunch, afternoon tea and dinner. We were up and down between the boarding house and the beach like yo-yos.

Anne McCormick, growing up in Speke, which was then still quite rural, enjoyed the contrast of visits to her family:

> We would go and stay with our cousins sometimes in Walton and I recall lying in bed listening to the milkman coming round in the morning with his horse and cart. Breakfast would be lovely porridge made by Auntie Elsie, or salt fish cooked by Auntie Emily. Both had toilets in the backyard and sheets of newspaper hanging on a string.
>
> We had one holiday with my parents when I was about fourteen. Dad got a loan from the bank and we went to Pontin's Middleton Towers in Morecambe. The sun shone every day, and I danced there every night to the jukebox and Dion & the Belmonts. Magic!

Doreen Stock, *née* Burton, was born in 1939 and lived in London until she was fifteen. She enjoyed holidays on Merseyside:

> My father's Aunt Annie lived in Birkenhead and we visited at least once a year for a holiday. We took the bus or ferry to New Brighton, which was exciting! The fair was a must, so much to do,

*Doreen Stock had a 'super time' on holiday with Aunt Annie and cousins on Anglesey!*

penny slot machines, helter-skelter and my favourite – the dodgem cars. Then sandwiches and a bottle of lemonade on the beach; in and out of the paddling pool and it never seemed to rain!

Another day we got the ferry boat to Liverpool – clasping my penny in my hand, I got my own ticket from the machine. With my mum and dad, Winifred and William, I visited the museum and art gallery. My favourite was St John's Market to see the old pets' corner. I was encouraged away by the promise of a cream cake in one of the many Lyons tea shops.

After Doreen's father died in 1952, her mother had to work:

When school holidays came, my mum would put me on a coach and sit me next to a lady and ask her if she would look after me. I spent most of my school holidays with my Aunt Annie. One year, we went to Anglesey with her cousin, Emily and her children, staying on a farm. What a super time that was!

My mum would come to collect me, travelling by Crosville coach overnight from London, which took ten hours, so she could have a two-day break. It was on one of these journeys that she met a Liverpool man and a friendship started. In 1954, they decided to marry and we moved to Liverpool.

Children enjoyed travelling alone to stay with relations, which gave them some independence. Mary Allport remembers some quite lengthy spells away from her parents, brothers and sister:

My dad was Scottish; he was a wonderful dad, always happy and loving, and I had a wonderful childhood between Liverpool and Scotland. My dad came from a place called Kilsyth. I used to travel on the Caledonian buses to Glasgow. I was left in the charge of the bus conductor. He would ask a couple to see that when the bus stopped I had lunch and they would look after me. Everyone was very kind. I would get to Glasgow, and Gran and Granddad would meet me off the bus. The journey then took about ten hours because it went right through the countryside.

When I was at Kilsyth I loved it. I was the first grandchild, so nothing was too good for me. Sometimes I would tell my mum and dad that I wanted to stay in Kilsyth, and Gran and Granddad would get me into St Patrick's School and I would spend twelve months there. I did that a couple of times. But then I would want to come home because I missed my mam and dad and, by this time, one sister and four brothers.

Margaret Gillson was happy living in Thirlmere Road, within sound of the roar of the Kop, but also enjoyed visiting Kent:

> I was lucky enough to spend summer holidays with an aunt and uncle in Kent. I was put in charge of the Guard and used to sit in the Guard's van. I was always quite safe and my uncle used to pick me up at Euston station. He was a clergyman and lived in a vicarage with a huge garden. We lived in a terraced house with outside loo, no bathroom and a cellar. When we went down in the dark for coal, we had a rolled lit newspaper and had to shovel the coal and run up the steps before it burnt out. You can imagine their house seemed like a palace to me!

Christine Deed also remembers travelling independently:

> We would often go by train to Manchester to see my grandma, auntie and uncle and cousins. By 1959, I was making this journey on my own and I thought of this as a holiday. Their house was in Fallowfield. We went to the park, 'the pictures', a jumble sale, the library and had a trip into Manchester with Grandma to see a £2,500 bed in Lewis's – it had mink covers.

For other children, the school provided their first holiday without their parents.
Chris Brocklehurst was one whose first holiday was with his school:

> When I was in the seniors, we went to the Isle of Man for a week. It was my first holiday ever! We slept on stretchers in a church hall in Peel. We got washed in cold water outside and some of the teachers cooked the meal for us with what we had brought with us. We also had to make our own sleeping bags. We took a blanket to school and we had to fold it to make an oblong shape, then we had to sew along one side and across the bottom and that was our sleeping bag. When we came home the stitches were removed to return it to its full size.

Colomendy Camp at Loggerheads, near Mold in North Wales, was originally built in 1939 by the National Camps Corporation as a wartime refuge for the schoolchildren of Liverpool. Since the end of the war, it has been visited by more than 350,000 children on holiday. Most of these visitors come from Liverpool, but there are the famous international camps too. Colomendy was leased by Liverpool after the war and bought in 1957 from the National Camps Corporation.
Harold Russell, like many other Liverpool schoolchildren, had his first taste of independence there:

> My first holiday without Mum and Dad was a week with Roscoe School to Colomendy Camp at Loggerheads. My two main memories of the week were that there were other nationalities at the camp and we had an organised football game – England versus The Rest of the World and I played for England. The other memory is that I wrote a letter to my mum telling her that we had white stuff with green dots all over our fish for dinner. It was parsley sauce, of course, but I didn't know what it was then!

Harold's younger brother, David, also went to Colomendy Camp:

> It was the last year in primary school and we could go to Colomendy in Wales for a week. I had never been away from home without my mum and dad, but I don't remember being worried about it.
> When we arrived, I was put in a boys' dormitory with all my classmates. I can't remember whether we were in bunks or not, but I do remember having to make my own bed in the morning and being told how to 'box your blankets' to make a neatly made bed.

During the day we went on nature walks around the grounds of Colomendy and the surrounding area. One day, towards the end of the week, we were taken to Loggerheads and could buy presents. I remember going into Woolworths and buying my mum four 'gold' egg cups – they were plastic! I can't remember whether I bought anything separate for my dad and brother or whether they had to share. However, the gold egg cups found their way into the display cabinet in the front room!

My mum was a good cook and I enjoyed her home cooking. It came as a shock to have the food at Colomendy, particularly the breakfasts. I can remember telling my mum and dad about the streaky bacon with no meat in it, the lumpy porridge and the greasy fried bread. But I survived and it was another brick in the wall in learning about life and living with other people.

Eileen Pritchard remembers, without any redeeming features: 'going to Colomendy Camp in North Wales with the junior school for a long weekend – I hated every minute of it; it was very cold; the dormitory was freezing; the showers were freezing and the food was awful.'

Gill Shaw remembers Colomendy too, but with very different feelings from Eileen:

I loved it – sleeping in the top bunk, the outdoor pool full of daddy-long-legs, the tuck shop, the totem poles, climbing Moel Famau and drinking from the streams, coming home on the coach with a tape measure that curled back up when you pushed a button, and a red plastic mouse for my cat. Mum had my favourite meal ready – fish fingers and a packet of crisps – and my Bunty comic!

# 8

# OUT AND ABOUT!

Robin Bird remembers the excitement that his father, Bob Bird's, profession as a photographer brought into his life even before he went to live in New Brighton:

*Miss New Brighton contestants: most resorts had a beauty contest and they were very popular at the time.*

*The Empress of Canada in 1953 after the fire aboard.*

Dad worked long hours and often did not get home until after we were in bed and asleep. However, he would take us to New Brighton during the summer holidays to attend the Miss New Brighton contest at the Bathing Pool. My mother and sister did not always come. On such occasions my father would leave me with the mothers of the contestants, getting the girls ready. He was busy taking photographs. At the end of the contest, we rushed off to get the negatives to the *Daily Post* and *Echo* or the *Evening Express* offices.

I seemed to wait hours in the car for my Dad to return from the newspaper's offices. Later, as a Cub reporter, I would work with dad on the Miss New Brighton contests, which were very popular events. Except for this boring part, the journey to and from New Brighton was a huge adventure for me, in the back seat, looking out at the dockland scenes, the Overhead Railway and the burned-out *Empress of Canada*. This wrecked liner on its side made a big impact on me as a child!

The Canadian Pacific liner, *Empress of Canada*, was launched in 1928 as the *Duchess of Richmond*; she underwent huge refurbishment at Fairfields of Glasgow, re-emerging in 1947 with her new title. She then had a refit before the Coronation, and was moved from the dry dock to the No. 1 Branch of the Gladstone Dock on 24 January 1953. She was fully booked to bring passengers from Canada to attend the Coronation, but, on the afternoon of the 25th, smoke was noticed by shore-side workers, who assumed that the welders were still at work. By 4.15 p.m., the fire had taken hold and was seen by those on board; the Bootle Fire Brigade was called. They believed that they were bringing the fire under control but dock and shipping experts decided to stop fighting the fire in the hope that it would burn itself out. This did not happen and the ship finally toppled over, leaving her starboard side visible. This is the sight that made such an impression on young Robin Bird!

Anne Orme, one of five children living in Waterloo, remembers that the river played a very important part in the life of her family; her father's homecomings were special occasions:

> Our father was a Chief Steward on the big liners and when he was due to come home, we would all run down to the beach and watch his ship sail up the Mersey and wave like mad! He always said that he could see us and that he waved back to us and we firmly believed this to be true.

Michael Moran also has vivid memories of the river:

> I used to watch the big ships sailing up the Mersey and the dredgers that kept it clear of sand. I saw fishing boats and shrimpers with their nets bulging with their catches. The *Royal Daffodil* was one ferry that I remember well, but I remember the *Royal Iris* most because she looked so majestic when she sailed past us on the River Mersey.

Michael, growing up in Speke, has memories of the airport: 'I remember going to an air show at Speke Airport to see the Fairey Delta 2 (FD2), a huge new aircraft. I think it was the first jet I had ever seen.' The Fairey Delta 2 was a research craft built by Fairey, at the request of the Ministry of Supply, to investigate the possibilities and requirements of supersonic flight. It must have been an impressive sight.

For many children growing up on Merseyside in the 1950s, a holiday was, by no means, an annual event; Michael recalls:

> We had one holiday at Butlin's, but mostly we went on day trips to New Brighton or West Kirby, when we travelled by bus and ferry from the Pier Head. We had picnics on the benches in Sefton Park, where we would watch the peacocks and quail running about us. Our picnics were mainly jam butties and for a drink we had water, usually in an empty pop bottle. I still remember the fright I had when one of the peacocks opened up its tail into a huge fan. The pattern on its tail looked just like a lot of eyes staring at me and I ran away screaming to my mum and dad. Sefton Park was beautiful and we would walk for hours amongst flowers and well-trimmed hedgerows; sometimes, if Dad could afford it, we would go out in a rowing boat for 1s 6d – the motorboats were more expensive, they were half a crown.

Janice Pickthall remembers local parks making it possible to enjoy precious free time together:

> My dad was a grocer and managed a shop in Rice Lane, cycling to work Monday to Saturday with half-day closing on Wednesday, so we would only have Sunday to enjoy as a family. Sometimes we would go to Walton Hall Park boating lake or the open-air theatre for talent shows, and sometimes there were brass band concerts.

Shirley Evans remembers fishing trips to the local park with her mother:

> In the school holidays, Mum used to take my younger brother and me to Newsham Park where we used to catch fish in the small pond there. Mum used to make us fishing nets out of old nylon stockings, a piece of wire and a garden cane.

*Myself and my little sister, Janet, enjoying a day at Waterloo beach, 1955.*

But Shirley also spent a lot of time with her grandparents, Thomas and Mabel Jones, who lived only four doors from her own home in July Road. Shirley's granddad took part in more serious fishing:

Sunday with Gran and Granddad was out with the fishing club. They would fish the rivers and canals all over Cheshire and Wales. Gran and I would walk for miles with the other wives, and when in season, picking blackberries.

Janet Arnot remembers that trips to the seaside did not involve travelling long distances:

My parents used to take us to Blundellsands beach, where we would build sandcastles and Dad would help to dig out boats and cars in the sand for us to play in. We had a large wooden case that was used to carry our picnic. The case was made by our father and when it was empty, it opened out flat to make a firm surface for the food and drinks. The sandwiches really were sand-wiches as they were always gritty because it was impossible to get all the sand off our hands, but I remember those days as happy times. Dad had a Box Brownie camera that had a canvas case with a leather strap, so it could be carried over his shoulder. He kept that camera all his life.

Gloria Nall also remembers Blundellsands:

I enjoyed going to the shore most Sundays. My mother would prepare a huge pack of sandwiches and fruit pies, flask of milk, teapot etc. This would all be packed in my two younger brothers' high pram; we would then walk to the station to board the train to Blundellsands, then get off and walk to the superb shore. I would take our huge teapot to one of the nearby cottages, pay sixpence and have it filled with boiling water on the dry tea inside. A lovely fresh-air sunny day and we never had to think about what the weather would be like – always a warm, sunny day!

Sue Jones, living in Lydiate, on the edge of open country, remembers:

Most summer Sundays we would go on a family bike ride after Sunday School, and usually have a picnic tea – summer always seemed to mean long sunny days in years gone by – or is that just my imagination?

Sue also remembers trips later in the year:

Another popular outing would be to see Blackpool Illuminations, organised by the PTA. We would board the bus outside school in the late afternoon so as to get to Blackpool to join the queue to proceed through the lights – what wonderful tableaux we saw! But part of the fun was not getting home until after midnight – I remember one occasion when we arrived back just before midnight and were walking home from the school when all the street lights went out and, to us children, we couldn't believe how dark it was.

Margaret Dunford remembers travelling with a purpose:

I was in a morris dancing troupe when I was about eleven. It was great! Every Saturday we would travel to competitions.

Dougie Cox enjoyed 'days out':

We went across the river to Seacombe on the ferry. At weekends we managed to get to the Pier Head, Sefton Park and Newsham Park, thanks to penny returns on trams and buses.

John Halley's favourite form of transport was the train:

From the end of Elton Avenue, Netherton, where I lived, you could see the two railway lines, one to Ormskirk and the other to Southport, now part of the Cheshire Lines. I loved watching the train peel away into the distance, following the curve of the rail. In the days of steam locomotion, my friend and I went all over the north-west trainspotting.

Lilian Williams also remembers the excitement of steam trains:

My favourite walk was to stand on a wire-mesh sided bridge near Kirkdale or Bank Hall to wait for the trains to envelop me in a haunting cloud of steam.

Holidays by train started with the wonderful aroma of coal and grease and the sound of hissing and chuff, chuff, chuffing as raw power moved the trains.

Christine Deed kept a diary for many years when she was growing up, so her memories are quite detailed:

Our family did not own a car but we borrowed one belonging to a family friend and our holidays in the summer usually consisted of 'days out' over a set period of a week or two weeks, always in Wales and the North West. I remember looking forward to these times with as much anticipation as if we had been going further afield.

In August 1958, we spent five days in Ainsdale, driving there each day. Eating out was a treat and we had our dinner at Whitehead's in the village. I nearly always had baked beans on toast on these occasions and they had to be Heinz: I refused to eat anyone else's. And the apple pie was never as good as Mum's.

We went to Southport one evening – the Land of the Little People and the waxworks. We never went to Southport beach – miles to the sea and indifferent sand-hills.

The next six days saw us mainly at Ffrith beach near Prestatyn with one day at Chester Zoo and one at Rudyard Lake. We loved Ffrith because it had penny slot machines and we spent a long time on them with the 2s Dad gave us, so it must have been quite easy to win. There was a boating lake with canoes and paddle boats, a helter-skelter, mini-golf and swings.

In 1959, the official holiday with the car lasted just a week, with day trips to Ainsdale and Freshfield. We really did spend most of the day on the beach, in all weathers – as long as it wasn't raining. We based ourselves at the same spot in the sand-hills each day and sometimes had a picnic with tea made using a Primus stove. Castles and moats were dug, dams built and we swam. The area behind the sand-hills at Ainsdale was full of birds and flowers and I recorded that we saw a skylark's nest with three eggs in it.

Joan Munro also remembers happy days at Ainsdale:

As my dad owned a shop on the corner of Vicar Road, we could only go out as a family on a Sunday. We would go in his van to Ainsdale beach. Mum would cook the joint of meat and take it along with bread and butter, tinned fruit and evaporated milk. She would make sandwiches when we arrived. Dad would take forever to light his Primus stove to boil a kettle for their cup of tea.

Patricia Gilbert was one of a happy family of seven children, so there was not much money: 'We never went on holiday. Our big treat was a day out to Chester Zoo. We all sat in a circle and our mum would get us all an ice-cream cornet.'

Chris Brocklehurst looks back on 'simple carefree days' with his family:

When we were on summer holidays from school, we would go pea-picking. The night before we went, my mother would get everything ready – tea and sugar mixed and condensed milk, which we called conny-onny, and some diluted orange juice. Some of the family were working, but those of us who were of school age would get up at 4 or 4.30 in the morning, and we would walk up Mill Lane to the Picton Clock and get the first Crosville bus to the Bridge Inn at Gateacre and then walk up to Capstick's farmhouse. The farmer would take us to the field, where he wanted us to work, on his cart.

For every hamper we filled we would get a tally. We would take the hamper that we had filled to the scales on the cart, where it was emptied into another hamper to make sure that you had not put stones in the bottom. At dinner time, the farmer would bring hot water round so your mum could make tea in the billy-cans. When we finished for the day, we would go up to the farmhouse to wash up and our mother would give the tallies in, for which she would get half a crown for each tally.

A half-crown was 2*s* 6*d* or thirty old pennies. It was an eighth of a pound or 25p. There were 20*s* in an old pound, so a shilling is today's 5p.

Chris continues:

Before we left the field we were told to fill as many bags as we could with peas; when we got home my mother would sell them to the neighbours for extra money. It was the same when we went spud-picking. We also went to West Kirby as a family, except for those at work. Again, before we left we were told to pack as many bags as we could with cockles. When we got home my mother would put a couple of big black pans on the stove and boil them and, again, sell them to the neighbours for a shilling for a big mug full.

We also went to Moreton. We got the train from Central station; the walk down from the station at Moreton to the shore at the bottom was all fields to run through. There was a caravan at the bottom where you could get a pot of tea for half a crown, but you had to leave another half-crown as a deposit to return the teapot and cups. There was also a small cabin where you could get hot water, so we always took our own tea, sugar, conny-onny and diluted orange juice. We also had a small tent that the girls could get changed in.

Gordon Crompton recalls working on a family farm:

Brown's Farm in Dingle Vale, off Dingle Lane, was a haven to me, having been introduced to my third cousin, Ken, who had been orphaned and lived there with his great-uncle, Albert Brown, and Aunt Chris, in a massive house, more like a mansion with two huge pillars in the front, just like the Mansion House in Calderstones Park.

My uncle used to get us working in the orchard collecting rhubarb and selling it to a local grocer for 2*d* or 3*d* per lb, and woe betide us if we didn't give him the right money after the sale, because he weighed it personally before we took it to the shop. I never got a single penny off him, but that didn't

*Christine McGarry at Prestatyn fairground.*

matter as I just loved going to the farm. On one occasion I ate a whole bed of strawberries – I didn't eat strawberries for years after!

Margaret Gillson's family enjoyed time together: 'The whole family – grandma, aunties, uncles, cousins – used to go to New Brighton for the day. We would all sit on the beach with pots of tea which could be purchased and brought onto the beach!'

Robin Bird recounts an amazing coincidence:

My dad was in partnership with Keith Medley with a photographic studio in King Street, Wallasey. Both men had been airborne photographers in the Second World War. They also had a photo booth at New Brighton called Walkie Photos. Hundreds of people enjoyed having a souvenir photograph of a 'day out' – one such anonymous little girl snapped by Bob Bird was Carla Pierpoint, who, many years later, became Bob's daughter-in-law, when she married me. But it was many years before we found the old photo with my dad's stamp on the back!

Like Chris Brocklehurst, William Duvall remembers West Kirby with affection:

I have said we had a hard upbringing and it was, but we always had holidays and days out. West Kirby was a quick day out and a short trip; but with up to eight kids in tow, it could not have

*Carla Pierpoint, aged five, with her mother Betty (left), cousin Bernard and Auntie Olive, photographed by her future father-in-law, Bob Bird. In the background, his colleague calls another family to be photographed.*

been easy and probably very trying. Dad did not go on these trips, just us and some cousins with our stepmother and an auntie or two. West Kirby was all beach, or so it seemed then. The train ride was great fun, part underground and part in the open. Pilchard butties or salmon butties – paste! I never saw a real salmon until I started work in Tesco. We always came home burnt from top to bottom; thank God for calamine lotion. As we got older, into our early teens, we often went our own way. New Brighton was the place to go from the old landing stage to the long-gone pier across the river. Fort Perch was fascinating, full of stuff from the war, just what boys wanted to see. We were told the big ovens were from the death camp – as kids we believed it to be true, such innocence!

Agnes Jones recalls special times with a group of young friends:

In my late teens, a huge part of my life was a social and travel club called The Country Friends. We met over a café in London Road every Monday. On Sundays, we'd go walking in Wirral, but we didn't push ourselves. No one had a car and we had to get to the ferry and get a bus to wherever we were going. The journey was an enjoyable part of the outing. A favourite place was Chester and I can remember one Sunday we hired a boat and rowed up the river all day. It was one of those sun-drenched happy days you always remember. I also treasure memories of a wonderful day out to Blackpool – the fairground and fish and chips in a café.

Anne McCormick shares the pleasure of days out:

We did not go on many holidays but had our bikes as we got older. We cycled all day, mainly in Speke but also to Hale Village. One memory I have is when a neighbour hired a car for a week or two and took me with his two daughters – my friends – to Blackpool for the day. Cliff Richard was Number One with Living Doll and it was playing on the waltzers. The sun was shining and it was marvellous. I was about twelve, I think. New Brighton baths was a real treat and my parents would take us there with friends and family. I can still smell the baths now. Some Sundays, my friends and I would get the bus ourselves to different places. Maybe only Lime Street station, where you could use a machine and make yourself a metal luggage tag with your name on. Or it may be just going over the Mersey on the *Royal Iris* and back again. We were quite independent from a young age and could go off for the day without our parents worrying about us.

Often 'days out' were enhanced by using the booklets that comprised the I-Spy series. The I-Spy books were very popular in the 1950s and thousands of children used these small volumes that encouraged them to be observant. Each of the books covered a different subject, such as *Cars*, *Trains*, *Churches* and *Letterboxes*. As a child spotted various items, they recorded the event in their own little book and gained points. When a book was completed, it could be sent to Big Chief I-Spy for a feather and order of merit.

Many children firmly believed in the Red Indian, Big Chief I-Spy, who lived in the Wigwam-by-the-Water or the Wigwam-by-the-Green. The original Big Chief I-Spy was Charles Warrell, a former headmaster, who created I-Spy towards the end of his working life.

Some children just used and enjoyed the books, but many joined the I-Spy club. Members of the I-Spy Tribe were called Redskins. There was an I-Spy button badge, proudly worn by members so that they could recognise one another and make friends.

# 9

# CHRISTMAS AND WINTER PASTIMES

Graeme Arnot remembers:

Christmas was very warm and full of fun. It was the only time of year that we had a fire in the front room as well as the back room, and there was always plenty to eat. I got the usual orange and tangerine and chocolate money. Also a Beano annual and small items that weren't very memorable. One year I got a joiner's kit with a plane and a saw and a hammer. When I was four, in 1955, Dad bought me a clockwork train set, a big one. It was second-hand but it was great! It didn't have much track. When I was seven, he sold it and bought me a Hornby Double oo train set; the following year I got a Meccano set, both of which I've still got.

My sister, Janet Arnot, also remembers childhood Christmases with affection:

At Christmas, the house was decorated and, in the hall, Dad put up lights that were bigger than normal Christmas tree lights and shaped like fruit. As a child, it felt like fairyland. Once, we had tree lights that flashed off and on intermittently; one evening we were having dinner and a man knocked at the door to tell us that our living room was on fire. He'd seen the flickering glow through the windows and thought that the flashing light was from flames.

I always had a pillowcase, instead of a stocking, for my presents. At the bottom, it always held an orange, an apple, a tangerine and a few new coins. I also got chocolate coins that came in a red mesh bag, a selection box, and, often, a jigsaw puzzle or game, or Plasticine for making models. I always got an annual. One year I came downstairs and, sticking out of the top of my pillowcase, was a beautiful doll; she was dressed as a bride and had dark hair, a veil, a silky dress, white shoes and socks and, unusually, imitation pearl earrings and necklace. She must have been about 18in tall and I loved her dearly for many years.

We always spent Boxing Day at my dad's sister's house. All the family went and Uncle Wal played the banjo; one cousin, young Walter, played the piano accordion and my Auntie Janey played the spoons and everyone danced. If the numbers were uneven, I remember my auntie danced with the mop! It was great fun and I never wanted it to be over.

Auntie Janey lived in Ladysmith Road, Fazakerley. She had moved in when the houses were built and, thirty years later, in the 1950s, there were still fields all the way down on both sides of Lower Lane, which was the way we usually approached her house. Fazakerley still seemed to be on the edge of the inhabited areas around Liverpool. This impression was reinforced by the fact that Janey kept chickens and had a run in her garden. She was our father's oldest sibling and had taken her mother's place as the matriarch

*I met Father Christmas in Lewis's grotto, 1950.*

of his family. It was for this reason that we all gathered at her house on Boxing Day, without any prior discussion. We all knew that if we wanted to see the rest of 'the gang', that was where they would be. The other aunts and our mother, took along contributions for the tea and supper table, and that was where I had a taste of piccalilli for the first time. I needed lots of water to drink after that experience; because we never had it at home, I hadn't known what to expect!

A lot of families still made their own entertainment when they all got together, especially in the early 1950s. There were usually some of the adults who could play a musical instrument, and children who were having expensive music lessons were expected to make some sort of contribution to the evening's fun!

At the home of my father's other sister, Emma, who lived in Peveril Street, there was a piano and both of her children, my older cousins, Wal and Brenda, had piano lessons and played the piano well, spending a lot of their money when they started work on sheet music of popular songs. When there were parties at their home for their twenty-first birthdays, or when my auntie threw a 'do' when Wal came home on leave from his National Service, both of them would play all the popular songs of the time, like Buttons and Bows. Although a lot younger, I would take a turn with something like The Christmas Alphabet or Wonderful Copenhagen, but the cousin who could play for the adults to dance, practically any tune you could hum to her, was my cousin, May, who had never had a lesson but played by ear. There was a strong musical tradition in my father's family because his grandfather had been a professional violinist.

But we don't seem to have been unusual. Patricia Shaw remembers, for instance:

> We had good Christmases because we had a piano and our cousins came for lunch then we sang all sorts of songs with my uncle playing the piano; he was Scotch, so it was mainly Scotch songs. A lot of them, I think he made up as he went along; all good fun, and we had a good time, all eight of us kids. I remember my mother saved with a club all year round 2s 6d a week, which paid for the Christmas lunch. We went and collected this from a church hall. The goodies were in a large hessian bag and I remember the bag having five items – turkey, a tin of tea, a tin of biscuits, a Christmas pudding and a Christmas cake.
>
> The turkey legs would be sticking out of the bag as it still had all its feathers; when we got it home, mam would hang the turkey by its legs up in the back kitchen, then pluck it and clean it on Christmas Eve.

Eileen Pritchard remembers:

> My dad loved the music of pianist Winifred Atwell and was keen for me to play the piano. From the age of seven to twelve, I went to weekly piano lessons. I hated them. I had to practise for thirty minutes every day. We had a lovely piano with a lovely pitch, which I obviously did not appreciate at the time. The piano was in the parlour, the best room, and in the winter it was freezing. I used to wear a coat and gloves to keep warm when I was practising! The fire was only lit about twice a year in that room. Eventually, to the great disappointment of my father, I gave up the piano when I started secondary school and had homework to do. I regret it now!

Mary Parkin kept up her lessons:

> I learned to play the piano from age eleven and really loved it! Mum and Dad promised me a piano if I passed the scholarship and I attended lessons in Walton, having to get the bus there and back. It was quite a struggle for my parents to afford 7s 6d for each lesson every week, but they did. I eventually achieved Grade Five in piano exams and being a pianist helped a great deal when I eventually became a teacher.

June Buckley also has happy memories:

> We had a wonderful childhood and our home was always filled with laughter. For Christmas there was always one main present for each of us, plus an apple, orange and a new penny. I can remember getting a John Bull Printing Outfit and was thrilled with this.

Pat Gilbert remembers:

> … a wonderful childhood, although very poor. Mum made seven dozen mince pies on Christmas Eve. We would all go to Mass together. We would get one toy each – a pastry set or a sewing set, called Milady, with different coloured cottons. We would get an apple and a tangerine and play games around the table – blow football, cards, or snakes and ladders.

Joe Swindells especially remembers the anticipation:

> Christmas was always an exciting time for us kids, because of the presents we might get. In those days, the build-up to the big day started around the second week in December. Shop windows would be filled with toys and Christmas annuals. We would be chatting in class about what we had asked for from Father Christmas and we did believe in him then! We always looked forward to a trip to the grotto. Presents from the grotto would cost half a crown and were, mostly, dolls for the girls or something to do with cowboys for the boys. I remember my present one year was a plastic, covered wagon and I spent many a happy hour playing with it. The big shops used to vie with one another to make the best grotto. We usually went to the one in T.J. Hughes department store. We marvelled at the Dancing Waters or Pinky and Perky.

T.J. Hughes, like Lewis's and Owen Owen's, was a department store founded at the end of the nineteenth century. It has been affectionately known as TJs by generations of Liverpudlians.

Pinky and Perky were puppet pigs created by Jan and Vlasta Dalibor. They were first broadcast on the BBC in 1957 and became very popular. They were almost identical, but Pinky wore red clothes, while Perky wore blue – Perky also wore a hat because of the limitations of black and white television. Their voices were sung by Mike Sammes, who also voiced Ken Dodd's *Diddymen*.

Anne Orme remembers Christmas hospitality:

> One memory I have is that at Christmas time, our postman, George, used to be rather tipsy by the time he got to our house as, at every house he called on Christmas Day, he was given a sherry. He still delivered all his mail on time.

Pauline Bennett has sweet memories:

> Each year my dad would make toffee apples for the whole school – I can't remember whether this was at Christmas time, but I do remember that at Bonfire Night, we always had lots of fireworks. Dad would get £5 worth, which was a lot of money. Mum would go mad at him, saying that it was a waste of money. We had a bonfire in the entry and the fireworks were set off in the backyard.

Christine Deed remembers an extra cause for celebration at New Year:

> Dad went out every year just before midnight with the dog, a lump of coal, money and bread. 1 January was his birthday so it was a double celebration. Mum would make mince pies. We could hear the hooters from the ships in the Mersey at midnight.

Michael Moran remembers Bonfire Night on his estate in Speke:

> Bonfire Nights were brilliant because our new housing estate was surrounded by forests and all
> the kids in our road used to go out together to collect all the dead wood and bushes to burn on
> 5 November. It was a social thing too, because some mums would bring potatoes that we would
> throw into the glowing ash to cook. Some would bring sausages and bread to cook and toast in
> the flames. Then we would watch the fireworks being set off by our parents with lots of Oohs!
> and Aahs! as they went off – especially the rockets!

Madeleine Roberts remembers that Bonfire Night in Kirkby was also a community occasion: 'All the
street celebrated Bonfire Night; there was a bonfire built on the roundabout at the top of the road. My
mum used to make treacle toffee for anyone who wanted it and it was all always eaten!'

Joan Gillett lived in Diana Street:

> Everton Football Ground was at one end of the street and, on Guy Fawkes' Night, a huge bonfire
> was lit in the shadow of the ground. For weeks, the boys were collecting old unwanted furniture
> and a Guy was placed on top of them. We used to roast potatoes in the embers of the blazing fire.
> The boys would be setting off bangers and we girls liked the Catherine wheels and sparklers.
> Good fun was had by all – all the women in our street were addressed as 'Auntie' and were always
> there to look after us all. A golden age indeed!

Joe Swindells lived in Knowsley:

> Living near woodland, we always had an inexhaustible supply of wood for Bonfire Night. For weeks
> we would collect fallen branches and any other combustible material to make a huge fire. This took a
> lot of time each night after school. But we would guard our efforts closely because rivalry might mean
> that other kids might take what you had gathered so carefully. We made a special effort with our Guy
> Fawkes. And he really did look like the image of the gunpowder plotter. Fireworks were much simpler
> then. For half a crown you could buy a box containing rip-raps, Roman candles, rockets and Catherine
> wheels, and also you could buy packets of sparklers. On the night, we would all gather round as rockets
> zoomed into the air and Catherine wheels whizzed round, pinned to a wooden post. When we played
> out in winter, we would make a 'Winter Warmer'. This was an old food can with holes knocked in it and
> a length of wire attached. We would stuff it with twigs and paper and light it. Then we would swing it
> round in circles to keep it alight.
>
> Bonfire Night and Duck Apple Night were two happy and important occasions in a child's year.
> For Duck Apple, we would actually duck for apples in a bowl of water or try to bite them, with
> our eyes closed, as they dangled from a string. No such thing as Trick or Treat then – everything
> was just innocent fun!

Christine Deed also remembers Bonfire Night and Duck Apple Night:

> At home we always called it that – not Hallowe'en. We had bowls of water in the living room for the
> apples and we strung some up across the room to try and eat with hands behind backs. To be able
> to eat as many apples as we liked was a treat. We were usually only allowed 'a half-each-apple' a day,
> which I always thought of as one word, as in 'Can I have my half-each-apple now, please?' Sometimes
> we had chestnuts as well. On Bonfire Night, the backyard was the scene of our fireworks. Catherine
> Wheels nailed to a pole, rockets, Golden Rain and Roman candles.

Shirley Evans also remembers fun with the family: 'Halloween was celebrated in our house with
bob apple, making toffee apples and stringing apples up on the clothes rack.'

Janet Arnot remembers everyday winter pastimes:

We stayed indoors and read our books, played with dolls or packs of cards, usually Patience, Happy Families and Snap, or with board games, such as draughts or snakes and ladders or, in my case, my beloved doll's house. This was my favourite toy – the doll's house that my father made for me. It had a flat roof, painted with blackboard paint and cotton bobbins for wheels so I could move it around as it was larger than most bought doll's houses and the rooms were large so that little hands had room to manoeuvre. Outside was covered in brick printed paper with a red front door and imitation lead-light windows painted yellow and green; the doors and windows could be opened and closed. Inside was wallpapered and had carpets all made from off-cuts that were left over from decorating our house. It had all the usual furniture, but also a grand piano and, in the kitchen, there was a washing machine, which had a wringer on top with working rollers turned by a handle and a little fridge that was painted inside with various food stuffs and had a removable ice-tray and tiny milk bottles.

My dad was very good at woodwork, so I also had a farm with stables. Each week we went to the shops in County Road, Walton, where the library was. My favourite shop was Baker's, a newsagent's, which also sold books and toys, and I would buy an animal for my farm there most weeks, unless the one I wanted was too dear; then I'd have to wait until I'd saved enough. I also had a much-loved teddy bear and Mum knitted a red and white striped jumper and red shorts for him. My mum taught me to sew and knit, and if I was ill she'd buy a tray cloth with a printed pattern on it and some embroidery threads so that I'd have something useful to do to pass the time until I was better. I also liked those magic painting books that you needed only water for … you used a brush to wet the page and the colours would appear by 'magic', making the picture visible.

It was in winter and bad weather that the large back bedroom in the house in Stuart Road, Walton, which I was lucky enough to have as a playroom, really came into its own. In this room, my father, Alf Brown, built shelves for my books, jigsaws and games. I had my rocking horse and my doll's house and doll's cot up there. My father made me a little ironing board and maiden, and a little desk, and I had my blackboard (an old pastry board painted with black paint), and a very old-fashioned easel, left from an earlier generation.

All the furniture in this room was old-fashioned, having come from my grandparents' home, but it was sturdy and comfortable and we didn't need to be too careful with it. There was a padded ottoman to sit on and to keep things inside. And there was a large round pedestal table, which was big enough to put out a jigsaw and still have space to paint or write. I had hours of fun, playing in this room, with my friends, Gwyneth and Barbara Jones, who lived opposite to us. Later, we would be joined by their little sister, Olwyn, and, even later, my little sister, Janet.

We had a trunk full of Edwardian clothes that had belonged to my grandmother and her sisters and we used these for 'dressing up'. The dresses and wraps would probably be worth a lot of money now, and there were ivory fans, beaded bags and kid gloves amongst them, but I think we had the best value from them.

Sometimes, my mother would buy some tiny Hovis loaves and penny meringues from Sample's cake shop on County Road, and we would have a doll's tea-party.

When Norma White played indoors, it really was something special:

My Auntie Maggie had a general shop on the corner of the entry that cut through Claudia Street and also rented the house and shop we lived in, so that nobody would open in competition with her. So the shop was left like a time-capsule. Where other children had a make-believe shop, I spent many happy hours with all my friends playing in a real one. There were barley-twist shelves with all the big old glass sweet jars with their glass stoppers, though their delicious contents had long gone! There was a marble counter that we always called the bacon counter. The whole ceiling was covered with a big coloured picture. I used to lie on the floor gazing up at it. It was a country scene with a little girl, standing on a stile face-to-face with a bull, which had huge horns, and the little girl was saying, 'I like you better as Bovril!'

Norma also enjoyed craft, sewing and knitting:

My mother taught my friend and me to knit whilst we were still quite young and we would go to the wool shop and buy a few balls of rainbow wool to knit clothes for our dolls. My cousin and I were fond of embroidery and we would go to the haberdashery shop and buy a tray cloth or sideboard runner with a printed design. We would spend hours choosing skeins of coloured threads.

Linda Leaworthy recalls shared activities:

The girls in our street had boxes of beads which were made from broken necklaces of mums, aunties and nans, and we would spend ages swapping them! When we were stuck inside, my mum would make us cardboard dolls and let us cut up her catalogue to make clothes for them.

Janice Pickthall also remembers playing indoors: 'When the weather was bad, we would play in the lobby. We also played board games, like snakes and ladders, ludo, dominoes and tiddlywinks from a Compendium of Games.'
  Christine Deed remembers that:

… our friends came to the house and we had tea-parties with our dolls; we played Scoop – the newspaper board game. We rather cheekily put on little shows and charged our friends to come and look at our pets. Refreshments were provided! I was heavily into handicrafts. I still had my dolls to rather an embarrassingly late age, but, rather than playing with them, I was knitting and sewing clothes and spending my pocket money on wool and material. I bought patterns at jumble sales and copied them out into little notebooks. Grandma taught me to knit and the family certainly enjoyed the results of my efforts. Auntie Bette delighted in the lime green jumper I made for her – the colour was her choice, I have to say – and my cousin had her share as well.

Anne McCormick also enjoyed creative activities:

I used to have my own nature table in our bedroom, based on the tin trunk which my dad was issued with on demob from the Navy after the war. I would grow carrot heads and beans. I would stand pussy willow branches in water to preserve them. I collected wild flowers and pressed them and put them in books.
  I was knitting and making my own clothes from the age of about twelve, as lots of people did then. I have a photo of my friends and me in a home-knitted cardie with fringing, sticky-out skirts, beehives and stilettos, when we were only about thirteen years old.

Mary Parkin wonders what happened to her creations:

I learned to knit and crochet and would sit on the step outside the house and crochet blankets from small oddments of wool that Mum had left from her knitting. I don't remember what I did with them though!

# 10

# THE CORONATION AND OTHER CELEBRATIONS

Queen Elizabeth II was crowned on 2 June 1953, having acceded to the throne on 6 February 1952. King George VI had come to the throne on the abdication of his brother, Edward VIII, later known as the Duke of Windsor. Despite his earlier popularity, most people resented what was widely seen as Edward's dereliction of duty, deserting Kingdom, Empire and People for Wallis Simpson. This feeling was reinforced when the Second World War began and everyone else had to do their duty, including the royal family. His parents, the King and his Queen, later the Queen Mother, became symbols of the nation's united resistance to the Nazi aggressors. The King was sincerely mourned.

Maimie Finney recalls that she went to a concert at the Philharmonic Hall on the evening of 6 February 1952, when the whole audience was asked to stand while the orchestra played Nimrod from Elgar's Enigma Variations. Maimie remembers that tears were streaming down many people's faces.

Doreen Stock was especially sad: 'My Dad died in January 1952. Then, in February, King George died and the country, as well as my mum, was in mourning.'

Shirley Evans remembers that her headmaster tried to introduce a sense of continuity: 'I remember the day the King died. I was at school, and the headmaster came into our classroom and told us the news. He then told us all to stand and sing God Save the Queen.'

And the nation's heart warmed to the new young queen, with her handsome war-hero husband, and her two little children, Charles and Anne; the people were ready to wholeheartedly celebrate her Coronation.

*Sherwyn Road, Clubmoor: Terry Arnot is second from right on the back row with his brother, Graeme, third from right on the front row. The actress, Alison Steadman, is second from right, second row. Barry Davies is left at the end of the back row.*

Shirley continues:

> When the Coronation was announced, all the neighbours in the road held a meeting to organise decorating our houses and arranging a big street party. I joined others in making crepe-paper roses in red, white and blue to put into hanging baskets for the outside of everyone's house. Only two or three neighbours had a TV at that time, so it was a case of bring your own chair and squeeze in somewhere!

For many people, this event was a justification for indulging in the expense of a television set, still a new luxury item. It had originally been thought that the event was too solemn to be televised, and that the bright lights and the heat that they generated would make the occasion too demanding for the young queen. However, when the then prime minister, Winston Churchill, conveyed to Her Majesty that these were the views of the Cabinet, she is said to have politely pointed out that it was, after all, her Coronation and she felt that all the people should be able to share the occasion.

The overall TV coverage was organised by Peter Dimmock and the main commentator inside Westminster Abbey was Richard Dimbleby, father of broadcasters David and Jonathan. It has been suggested that Elizabeth II's Coronation ushered in the television age.

There were an estimated 20 million viewers, although many of these were crowded into a neighbour's house! However, the sale of TV licences rose by 50 per cent during the following twelve months. Many of these new viewers probably had their first sight of television because of the Coronation.

Eileen Kermode was one of these new viewers:

> My aunt and uncle lived in a bungalow in Crosby and had a very large lounge with a small bay at one end. There was a curtain that cut the bay off from the room.
>
> On 1 June there had been a lot of bustling around. The lounge had been moved about so that all the chairs faced the bay with its curtains, behind which I was not allowed to look! Extra chairs were brought in from the rest of the house. The furniture in the dining room was moved about so that the table was along one wall and the sideboard along another and trolleys by the window. The smell of polish pervaded the whole house.
>
> Then there was a lot of activity in the kitchen too, with sausage rolls, sandwiches, cakes and jellies being made. Glasses, cups and saucers, plates and dishes and cutlery were all washed and put on the sideboard in the dining room.
>
> On 2 June, everybody was up early and it seemed to me that it took as long to check that everything was in its correct place as it had to put it there the day before. At the end of May, Grandma and I had made a Coronation parade from printed card and had stuck it on short boards which were to be put on the long window ledge. The only thing that I still have is the Coronation coach which was golden plastic!
>
> Then I was dressed in a blue and white striped dress upon which Mum had sewn red buttons. Friends started to arrive and they and all the family were shepherded into the lounge. The curtains on the bay were drawn back and there was a box with doors on it! The doors were opened and we were astounded to see a wonderful 12in television. It was switched on and we waited – suddenly there was a picture – this amazed my grandma, who started to cry. She was actually able to watch the Coronation of this new young queen; she kept on saying, 'Poor young thing, she is too young to take on such responsibility.' Of course, I sat on the floor right by the television enjoying a front-row seat. What a wonderful experience! I still remember the smell and excitement of that day – the polish, the food, the tobacco; the men nearly all smoked pipes – not during the Coronation though!
>
> After the television was turned off, we all enjoyed a wonderful buffet – I do not think I had ever seen so much food – well, it was not long since the war had finished. It was a super day!

Pauline Bennett remembers being proud of her family's television set:

We had a 12in television in time to see the Coronation; many neighbours crowded in to watch the ceremony. My nannie and granddad had a 9in set enclosed within a polished wooden case; we thought ours was bigger and so much better!

We had a fancy-dress street party for the Coronation. My mum was one of the organisers and I would go with her each week to collect from the neighbours. She had a book with their names in it and marked up what they had paid.

I still have my Coronation mug and red propelling pencil with a crown on it, inscribed for the Coronation. All children received a mug; the pencil may have been a street-party present.

Christine Deed comments:

The Coronation in 1953 was memorable because of television. There were not many of them about in Walton at that time but Dad was technically-minded and had made ours from a kit. We had a sort of shield to tie round the screen to make the picture clearer. It sat in the corner of the room and neighbours came in to watch. Our friends returned the compliment a couple of years later when ITV arrived. Dad held out against it for a while – all those advertisements – and we had to go to friends' houses to keep up with the current favourite programmes.

Mike Formby went to a very small country school, which has since closed:

The family moved to Lydiate in 1948; there were six of us: my parents, myself and two young sisters – I gained a brother and two more sisters during the 1950s. From the age of five, I attended St Joseph's School in Hall Lane and I stayed there until I went to the grammar school in 1956. They say that you never forget a good teacher and the headmistress of that school was a very good teacher – her name was Moira Dundon and she lived in the adjoining schoolhouse.

At the Coronation in 1953, the headmistress arranged for a television to be put in one of the classrooms so that all the local people could come to watch – I went with my mother and grandmother, my sisters must have gone as well.

But television was not the only thing that made the Coronation celebrations memorable, especially for children. Mike also recalls:

After the ceremony, there was a tea party in the old St Thomas' School on Southport Road, Lydiate. All the schoolchildren got a book and a commemorative spoon, compliments of Lancashire Education Committee.

Bill Duvall was only three years old in 1953. But he has a very special reason for remembering Coronation Day:

One thing that stands out for me is the Coronation; it being on 2 June. It was a very happy day – a big street party as many will remember – for my part, being so young, I did not know about such things. My birthday was on 1 June, so I thought the party was for my birthday. It was a long time before I understood what all the fuss was about!

Janice Pickthall's birthday was 2 June:

I celebrated my sixth birthday on Coronation Day. I remember the streets being decorated with flags and bunting and some streets having parties, although we didn't have one in Kiddman Street.

We went to my Uncle Arthur's home in Orrell Park to watch the Coronation taking place, because he had a television, with a magnifier screen on a stand placed in front. I was given a few Coronation mugs, including the one that was given out to all the schoolchildren.

Eileen Pritchard was eight at the time of the Coronation:

The Queen's Coronation I remember vividly. My aunt and uncle, who lived across the road, were the first in the street to buy a television and we all crammed into the small living room; children on the floor, adults sitting or standing, and we stayed there all day marvelling at the magnificent costumes. Sandwiches and cakes were passed around at frequent intervals and we all had to be quiet to listen to the words being said. The screen was very small – about 12in.

We had a street party after the Coronation. Street parties were great fun; we had coloured string tied to our cutlery and initials put on our plates to identify our own. We played games and dressed up. Everyone was very friendly; even neighbours who generally argued were sociable for the day. I remember receiving a silver medal and a commemorative cup and saucer, which I still possess.

Joan Munro also remembers a special souvenir:

My parents put a lot of effort into decorating my doll's pram in red, white and blue, including my doll, and I, also dressed in red, white and blue, went along to Anfield Road School where all the girls' prams were decorated and the boys had decorated bicycles. I went to a street party in Feltwell Road – we had lots of jellies, cake and sandwiches and the girls were given a brooch in the shape of a crown, decorated with red, white and blue stones.

There was a street party in Bellamy Road, to which, because we lived in the much busier Stuart Road, my mother contributed so that my sister, Janet, and I, could attend. Other friends from

*Joan Munro in her Coronation Party costume, with her decorated doll's pram.*

*The May Day procession in Bellamy Road, Walton, Coronation year. From the front of the procession: Beryl Carr, Olwyn Jones, Rosemary Broadbent, Robert Radford, Doreen Carr, John Coventry, Joan Coventry, Adrienne Allen, Gwyneth Jones, as a daisy, holding the maypole, myself as a rosette, Philip Broadbent, Barbara Broadbent and Barbara Jones, as a buttercup.*

Bellamy Road and some from Stuart Road and Bedford Road were there too. I remember that it was a cold and damp afternoon, even when the rain had stopped, and my sister sat in her high chair at the long trestle table, with a paper crown on top of a woollen bonnet to keep her ears warm. She was fifteen months old.

My mother allowed me to join in the May Day procession that year. Each year, children informally 'dressed up' on May Day and walked around the streets with a collecting tin. Normally, my mother thought that this was nothing more than begging, and some of my friends' mothers thought so too, but that year we were all allowed to join in as the procession had a Coronation theme. I went as a rosette, all in red, white and blue. The May Queen was Beryl Carr, and the other children were Gwyneth, Barbara and Olwyn Jones, Doreen Carr, Adrienne Allen, Joan and John Coventry, Barbara, Philip and Rosemary Broadbent and Robert Radford. There was also a Walter Raleigh and a Francis Drake, as well as other patriotic costumes, two gypsies and a Maid Marian. We had a party in the Broadbent's backyard, which we fondly imagined had been paid for by our 'haul', but there was such a spread and so many homemade cakes and sandwiches that, obviously, our mothers had contributed generously!

Barbara Doran was thirteen in 1953 and lived in Toxteth Grove, Dingle. She remembers the Coronation celebrations there:

For weeks we were making paper roses and flowers from crêpe paper, curling the petals with knitting needles, and also flags and bunting were made and attached to string and were stretched from one bedroom window to the opposite side of the street to a neighbour's upstairs window. Every house had red, white and blue flowers around the downstairs front windows. I remember all the terraced houses and streets around Dingle were decorated in this way. My friend and I even painted the brick wall at the end of our Grove with the words 'Coronation HM Queen Elizabeth II 1953' in red, white and blue paint.

Harold Russell recalls the involvement of Liverpool's schoolchildren in the Coronation celebrations:

To commemorate the Queen's Coronation, I was lucky enough to be part of a mass gymnastics display at Goodison Park. All the Liverpool schools took part in this display and many rehearsals took place during the latter part of 1952 and early 1953. At the end of the display, a massive aerial view of EIIR was formed, with some children in white shirts and others in red or blue.

Dougie Cox lived in Layford Close, Huyton:

My mother, Teresa Cox, worked for Littlewoods Pools with two of her sisters, Vera and Lily; my stepfather, Thomas Cox, was a miner when the Coronation happened. We were a big family with four girls and four boys and we got on quite well for such a large family. We lived in the Close, which was a small community – twenty-five houses – of working class people: miners, dockers, clerks, builders and busmen.

When it was announced that the Queen was to be crowned in June 1953, all the parents decided to have a celebration to mark the occasion. They held meetings in one another's houses and raised a weekly subscription and organised a programme for the event. Nobody was really well off, but the adults of Layford Close did a great job for a great day!

Each house was decorated and lamp posts, gates and kerbs were painted red, white and blue. The children were eagerly awaiting the great day. We had a party and each child was given a Coronation mug and pen and various other treats. Afterwards we went on a hired double-decker Corporation bus to see the decorations and the sights in Liverpool. All in all, an eventful and glorious day. A lot is spoken these days about community spirit, but I reckon we saw it at its best in that small close in Huyton in 1953!

*Coronation Party in Layford Close, Huyton. There was a wonderful community spirit. Dougie Cox is third from the right in the back row.*

There were many other occasions for rejoicing! The Queen's wedding day in November 1947 is especially remembered by Shirley Evans, who remembers her parents providing a particularly treasured toy:

> Two particular toys I remember from my childhood are a doll for me and a tricycle for my brother. The tricycle was a large wheel three-wheeler with a bell that I remember Mum saving for. My younger brother loved it.
>
> The doll arrived for me from my dad the day the Queen got married. I can remember my dad bringing it into the house. It was an expensive doll at the time and they were hard to come by. It cost my dad seven guineas and she is called the 'Walkie Doll' as her body is stitched in such a way to allow her body to move. She has a china or pottery head with rolling eyes and pottery hands and feet. I still have her.

June Buckley remembers Empire Day as a special celebration: 'I can remember my mum making us all dresses in red, white and blue for Empire Day.'.

The first Empire Day was in 1902; the chosen date was 24 May, the birthday of Queen Victoria, who had died in 1901. It was intended to remind people, especially children, across the world, that they all belonged to the great family of the British Empire. Although it was not recognised officially until 1916, many schools across the British Empire were celebrating it before then.

Janet Arnot also remembers Empire Day: 'I remember wearing my Brownie uniform to school; other girls were wearing their uniforms and the boys wore their cub uniforms.'

Bobbie Binks remembers celebrations in Fazakerley: 'There were parades quite often at school; we were told to decorate our bikes and there were always decorated wagons and a queen was selected each year.'

The Festival of Britain is another special event remembered by the children of 1951. Pat Plunkett, *née* Hearty, was born in 1937:

> I remember that I was due to go to the Festival of Britain in 1951, with my school, which was St Francis de Sales in Hale Road, Walton. For some reason that I don't know, the school trip was cancelled.

In 1951, Liverpool enjoyed 'a Festival of the people for the people' – a spin-off from the Festival of Britain. It included theatre, music, opera, ballet and street pageants, processions and firework displays. It was intended that there should be something to interest everyone.

Enid Johnston comments:

> I remember the Festival of Britain, but was not able to go and see it. As we had no television in 1951, we saw it on the cinema newsreels or pictures in the newspapers, which mainly showed the Dome of Discovery and the futuristic rocket-shaped Skylon, which caught the imagination of everyone.

Eileen Kermode's school was in Maghull:

> The only thing I remember about the Festival of Britain was the day we went to Scott's Bakery. We walked down Dunningsbridge Road and joined a queue. I presume we were shown the mechanics of the bread making but I cannot remember that! We were given a Festival badge made of black plastic and covered with a golden paint, which I still have. Then the highlight – we were given a small brown loaf and not only did I like the look of it because it was small, I also liked the taste!

Bill Kermode's memory of the Festival of Britain centres on the pageant at St Bridget's CE school in Lawrence Road, in which he was dressed as a Norman knight, with a long tunic and a sword.

Very few children seem to have travelled from the Liverpool area to London for the Festival of Britain, although, like Bill, many of them were involved in local celebrations and events.

Hazel Rimmer was lucky enough to visit the Festival:

> I went to the Festival of Britain in 1951 with my school. The cost was £1 10s, a lot of money in those days. My parents paid 2s 6d weekly. On the day, we met up under the Lime Street clock at 8 a.m. for the London train. A double-decker bus picked us up on arrival and took us to the Festival. Afterwards we were taken by bus to see Buckingham Palace. I particularly remember the Festival lights at the end of the day, especially the illuminated Skylon. Its slim, cigar-shaped steel structure illuminated with tungsten lights seemed to glow in the dark. We went home on the midnight train and arrived at about 5 a.m. I was very tired but remember that, as I went upstairs to bed, my father was coming down to start his working day. School had allowed us half a day off to rest. We were supposed to come in at 1.30 p.m. but quite a lot of people took the whole day off!

Grahame Settle visited the Festival, but was not over-impressed:

> My mother had a cousin living just outside London, and consequently we were able to go to visit the Festival of Britain whilst staying there. The main excitement was to see the Skylon – but I can't recall exactly what it was! Some sort of tower, I think.

June Buckley remembers: 'A day when we celebrated Liverpool, singing all the shanty songs.'

Memorable though the celebrations for the Festival of Britain were, it is more likely that June, who was seven in 1957, remembers when Liverpool celebrated the 750th anniversary of King John granting the city its Borough status. This was the year when schoolchildren were each given a copy of *The Story of Liverpool*. The mood in 1950s Liverpool was generally optimistic, and the destruction in the same year of the Overhead Railway and the abandonment of the tram system were seen as progress at the time.

*Bill Kermode dressed as a Norman knight for the pageant at St Bridget's School to celebrate the Festival of Britain.*

# 11

# BROWNIES AND WOLF CUBS; SCOUTS AND GUIDES

Terry Arnot was born in December 1939 and lived in Sherwyn Road, Anfield. Terry recalls good times as a Scout:

Between 1950 and 1956, I was a member of the 5th Anfield (208th Liverpool) Scout Group, firstly as a Cub, then as a Boy Scout and, finally, as a Senior Scout. The Group Scoutmaster was Mr Don Suddick, who was always referred to as 'Skip'. Looking back, I realise now what a dedicated man Mr Suddick was. I never knew, or perhaps I have forgotten, what he did for a living, but he and his wife devoted a significant part of their lives, between these years and beyond, to the Boy Scout Movement in Liverpool. The front room of their house in Knocklaid Road, Tuebrook, was, at times, a storage room for the equipment of a Scout group. Tents of all sizes, camp cooking equipment, Scout band instruments, flags and many other items, took up much of the space of the room.

During my time, the group changed meeting places several times. Venues included Clubmoor Presbyterian church hall, Pinehurst Avenue Boys' School Hall and, for a short time, the recreation room of the Troy Laundry on Utting Avenue. As well as working for the various Cub and Scout badges, we had regular church parades, about once a month. Usually, we paraded to Clubmoor Presbyterian Church, at the junction of Cherry Lane and Townsend Lane, but, occasionally, we went to Anfield Methodist Church, which stood at the junction of Oakfield Road and Walton Breck Road. Our parade featured a band with a bass and kettle drums and cavalry trumpets. The parade was led by the Senior Scoutmaster, Mr Jim Clough, who also played the cavalry trumpet. The solo drummer was the Scoutmaster, Mr Jack Wildridge. Both the Union Flag and the flag of the 5th Anfield Scouts were carried, often with difficulty if there was a strong wind. Our routes were not confined to the main roads; we would march along side streets and through housing estates. More than once, an irate householder would appear and demand that we stopped making a row as we were disturbing the peace of Sunday morning. I was one of five or six Scouts who played the cavalry trumpet. Regular band practice was usually held before or after the Scout meetings, when new trumpet calls could be introduced. To improve our playing and avoid causing a nuisance, Barry Davies, a friend and fellow Scout, and I would sometimes take our instruments to the middle of Clubmoor Rec and blast away! Perhaps an unusual approach to rehearsal, but it was effective.

There were continual efforts to raise funds for the group. Gordon Forrest, another neighbour and friend from Scouts, and I spent many hours pushing a small hand cart around the streets between Pinehurst Avenue and Norris Green, knocking on doors and asking 'Please, have you any jam jars for the Scouts?' We collected hundreds. It was amazing how many people had hoarded used jars, presumably waiting for organisations like the Scouts to collect them. For our efforts, we were presented with a knife, fork and spoon set for use in camp.

For Bob-a-Job week, Gordon and I chopped, wrapped and then sold bundles of firewood. The wood, which came in the form of sections of large packing cases, was supplied by Gordon's father, who worked in Kardomah's tea-importing operation.

The Kardomah Coffee Company was founded in 1845 in Liverpool. In the early twentieth century, the company started opening cafés throughout the country. These were very successful, partly as 'respectable' meeting places for women. As late as the 1960s, they were still popular with young people, but the chain declined. Nevertheless, they were the forerunner of the modern chains,

*The 5th Anfield Scouts and Wolf Cubs outside Pinehurst Avenue School.*

such as Caffè Nero and Costa Coffee. In the fifties, they were a large concern and must have gone through a lot of tea chests!

Terry continues:

> We charged twopence (2*d*) per bundle for the firewood and, as we had no difficulty in selling all we could make, we were able to confine our activity to the immediate vicinity of Sherwyn Road. It could be argued that we were not really conforming to the spirit of Bob-a-Job week, but we made quite a lot of money and I don't remember anyone complaining.

Bob-a-Job week was one of the biggest events of the Boy Scout year. A 'Bob' was a shilling, then twelve pence. And for one week of the Easter school holiday, Scouts went all over the area, walking miles, knocking on doors and saying 'Hello, this is Bob-a-Job week; do you want any jobs done?'

Scouts took on tasks like cleaning out garages, walking pets, gardening, car washing, shopping, and so on, for a shilling. The Scouts had cards and the 'customer' had to fill in what job was done, how much was paid, and how well the job was done. The day finished in late afternoon, when the money was collected in at the Scout hut. It was a very tough week for Scouts, and it was worse in bad weather.

Some people were generous and supportive to the Scout Movement, and gave easy jobs and double or even treble the money. Some people gave a half-crown. Others did exploit the situation and gave a job that would last all day, without raising their contribution. Bob-a-Job week went on for many years, until it was decided that it should be changed to Scout Job week, as a shilling was no longer sensible for the work done. Times had changed too, and at many houses there was no one at home when the Scouts called, because women were out at work. Scouts began to do more 'sophisticated' jobs like bag packing and so on, and the money was a lot better. Recently, however, there have been suggestions that Bob-a-Job week is about to reappear in 2012 as Scout Community Action week.

As well as working hard, Terry remembers plenty of fun:

> Camping was always a popular and enjoyable part of the group's activities – the two-week summer camp being the highlight of the Scouting year. For a number of years we went to Hawarden in North Wales and camped on land which was, I believe, part of an estate that had once belonged to the Victorian prime minister, Mr W.E. Gladstone. On Sundays we would dress in uniform and parade to the village church. Our route would take us down country lanes and along the main street of the village. We did not take our band instruments but we did carry the flags. The congregation of the church gave us, as I remember, a guarded welcome, while retaining what I

believe was a degree of scepticism, or perhaps it was bewilderment, that a group of boys from Liverpool could really be attending divine service.

At other times, Whitsun and Easter, we would go to the Boy Scout Camping Ground at Tawd Vale, near Ormskirk. The daily routine at camp included cleaning the cooking and eating utensils, gathering firewood, games, badge work and generally attempting, but usually failing, to conform to the ideals and practices set out in Baden-Powell's book *Scouting for Boys*. Unlike the transport arrangements today, governed by Health and Safety regulations, we had a more relaxed approach. We travelled to and from camp by lorry. Both boys and Scoutmasters, together with all the kit-bags and camping equipment, were exposed to the elements, totally disregarding the possible dangers which, in this more progressive age, diligent bureaucrats have managed to identify.

Harold Russell, eighteen months older than Terry, was also a member of the 5th Anfield Scout Group:

I joined the 5th Anfield in the last couple of years of junior school, first as a Cub and then as a Scout. I went on many Scout camps, including a Jamboree at Tawd Vale, near Ormskirk in Lancashire. One of my friends in Scouts was Peter Shakeshaft, whose parents were friendly with my mum and dad. They all came to see us at the Jamboree camp and I remember sitting in the campfire circle with a totem pole in the middle and they were in the circle too, along with other visiting adults.

However, one of my best experiences with the Scouts was to be chosen to represent the local Scouts on a barge trip from Liverpool to Leeds along the Leeds & Liverpool Canal. We took a letter from the Lord Mayor of Liverpool to the Lord Mayor of Leeds. One of the leaders presented the letter to him at the end of our journey.

I went camping in England, Scotland and Wales, sometimes with Scouts and, at other times, with some of my mates. I think that camping with the Scouts had given us the confidence to go on our own.

Like Terry Arnot, Harold remembers Mr Suddick, the Scout leader:

One day, I was out on my bike with a pal. It was nothing to do with Scouts. We went to Raby Mere and I fell off my bike at the bottom of the steep hill there and badly lacerated my hand. The skin of the palm of my hand was hanging off and full of gravel. I don't know how I rode home and I still bear the scars! I didn't want my mother to see the state of my hand, so when I got back I went to Mr Suddick's house, which was near where I lived. He cleaned it up, got out the gravel and bandaged it for me, so that when I went home I didn't have to upset my mother.

Terry Arnot commented on the need for the 5th Anfield to move their meeting place on a number of occasions. This had unfortunate consequences for Harold's younger brother, David:

My brother, Harold, had been a Cub and was a Scout in the 1950s. Sometimes he used to bring home the flag on a Friday ready for Church Parade on Sunday and he used to go to camp. I really wanted to be a Cub and a Scout like him, but, unfortunately, the Scout leaders and Clubmoor Presbyterian Church, which my parents attended, fell out over something and the Scouts moved away, so I was not allowed to join. I have always regretted it.

Like David's family, Terry's family also attended Clubmoor Presbyterian Church; his younger brother, Graeme, born in 1951, comments: 'A lot of the children belonged to Scouts or the Church Lads' Brigade and this was very popular until about 1960, when the novelty seemed to wane and nobody was a member of these organisations.'

David does not remember any of his friends going to Cubs or Scouts either, so it appears that a whole group of children and young people in that area missed joining these groups – due in part to their removal from the church to a new meeting place.

Mary Parkin remembers fun in the Brownies:

I loved attending the Brownies at St Ambrose Church and remember Mrs Hesketh, the Brown Owl. We danced around a papier maché toadstool that had seen better days and the papier maché owl had seen better days too. I remember it kept falling off the spotted toadstool!

I think I was in the Fairies, who were 'bright and gay, helping others on their way' or the Elves, who were 'helping others, not ourselves' and was a Sixer. We learned to darn and do knots. I still use the reef knot to this day if I have to join two pieces of string together. We had displays for parents and did figure marching to the tune of Blaze Away – we'll make a bonfire of our troubles and we'll watch them blaze away! The Brownie badge had to be cleaned with Brasso every week.

I was a Brownie with the Walton Church Pack and, like Mary, remember cleaning my Brownie badge. It was important that the back of your badge was as clean as the front. Your badge represented your 'honour', and what was not seen was just as important as what was visible to the world – quite a good lesson for children to learn!

We sometimes had a fancy-dress party. I remember going as an elf to one party and to another, at Christmas, as a Christmas tree; I wore a green dress with little presents and toys stitched all over it and a green crêpe paper pointed hat with a star on top! I won a consolation prize, which was a cardboard box of toffees. The box had little people on it, whose legs and bodies and hats changed as you slid the toffees out. I had the box for years and never tired of it. It fell to pieces in the end!

Friday night was Brownie night and, in order to get to Brownies on time, I had to have my tea early, rather than waiting until my father got home from work to eat dinner together. So my mother, who was not usually a fan of 'bought' chips, would send me to Byrne's fish and chip shop, on the opposite corner of the crossroads of Stuart Road and Bedford Road, for fourpenn'orth of chips, with which she would fry me an egg. I used to enjoy my egg and chips on Fridays – it was an extra treat that was always linked with Brownies!

*Walton Church Brownies, fancy-dress party, 1953. Back row from left, Gwyneth Jones, Pat Woods, myself, and far right, Barbara Jones.*

Joan Munro flew up to Guides and remembers being told: 'As a Brownie, you have done great things; fly up to Guides and do greater things!' Joan went on in Guiding and was for many years a much-loved Brown Owl.

Eileen Kermode, who later became Captain of the 1st Maghull Guides, had always been aware of Guiding, because of the involvement of her mother and her aunt:

> I joined Brownies with three of my friends. My Auntie Eileen, who was a Commissioner in Aintree and a friend of Brown Owl, came along to the Brownie meeting and we four made our Brownie Promise and she pinned on our badges. We sometimes met in the parish Institute and sometimes in the school. We used to play on Pimbley's playing field during the summer and look for four-leaved clovers and other interesting plants and insects. There were many hairy caterpillars in the hedge, and, although we were told not to touch them, we would have races with them!
>
> I flew up into Guides when I was eleven and joined the Swallow Patrol. My Patrol Leader was Gill Mason and now, over fifty years later, we are still good friends and still in Guiding! Later, I was Patrol Second of the Kingfisher Patrol but returned to the Swallows to be Patrol Leader. In 1954, I went to London and stayed at Our Ark, the Guide hostel in London.

Our Ark (1939–1959) preceded Pax Lodge in Hampstead as the London Centre of the World Association of Girl Guides and Girl Scouts (WAGGGS). Eileen continues:

> We went to camp each year at the end of August when Captain considered that, as it went dark by nine, we would all want to be in our beds by that time, as there was nothing to see or do outside our tents! Camps would take place in North Wales or the Lake District. I recall the furniture van outside Maghull Parish Institute being packed with our camping equipment, our rucksacks, bedding and food. We Guides would get in last and as we drove along we would hang over the loading board calling to drivers, and singing campfire songs all the way to the site. The first camp I went on was to Windermere and we had a super week of sunshine, when we did all sorts of crafts and games and had an enjoyable visit into the town.
>
> In 1955, the camp was in North Wales; we pitched the tents in a field where there was a stream. We used to wash our pots in the stream and then rinse them in fresh water. It was during this week that, due to heavy rain, we actually dug trenches around our tents so that water would not encroach on our beds, and we would sleep dry inside. It was at this camp that we learned that 'if you cannot camp in rain – you cannot camp!'
>
> In 1956, we went to the Lake District and arrived at the farm just as the rain started and the wind began to blow. We pitched the tents and lit the fire, but the rain got heavier and the younger Guides were sent into the marquee to keep dry while the older ones tried to cook dinner under a smoke shelter. After dinner, the wind got worse and the rain poured down so that the ground became very sodden and pegs started to come out of the ground. A decision was made that the Guides would sleep in the shippen over the sheep, in a warm and dry but smelly situation! During the night, the storm raged and the marquee roof ripped right across. When we woke in the morning, everything was very damp and as we put on our wellies a tiny mouse ran out of one.

Pauline Bennett also remembers wet weather camping:

> I went to St Oswald's Guides in Old Swan with a friend; we walked there and back, stopping for chips and a drink on the way home. We went camping once to Holmes Chapel, travelling in the back of a furniture lorry. My sleeping bag was a folded blanket, fastened with safety pins. On the third night at the camp, there was torrential rain and we had to gather our belongings and walk across the wet field to the barn for the night. We had to be sent home by train the next day as the conditions were too wet!

Patricia Gilbert recalls:

> When I was in the Guides, I had the chance to go away. Dad said I couldn't go as we hadn't the money. I cried all night. Next day, Dad won some money on the horses. I can see him vaulting over the back gate and producing two shiny half-crowns. I could then go on my holiday to Shrewsbury!

Chris Brocklehurst also went to St Oswald's Church: 'I joined the Cubs – the 13th Fairfield. We would meet in the church hall. Later I joined the Scouts. I think that helped me to do what I did later in life.'

Shirley Evans is one of the vast numbers of people who make it possible for children to enjoy Cubs and Brownies, Guides and Scouts:

> I joined the Girl Guides when I was twelve at Holy Trinity Church, Breck Road. I was in the 'Forget Me Not' patrol, but I didn't stay long as I became a helper for the Cub Scouts at the Free Church of England, Tuebrook. I stayed there for twelve years, eventually becoming one of the leaders.

Bill Fitzgerald recalls a memorable holiday and the people who made it possible:

> In 1950 when I was ten years old, I went with a couple of classmates from Beach Road School in Litherland to join the 2nd Crosby Sea Scouts.
>
> Two years later, we were invited to go to summer camp which was to take place in the Lake District. So in the weeks leading up to the big day, it was off to the Army and Navy surplus store, in Byrom Street, to buy a kit-bag, groundsheet and enamel mug and plates.
>
> On the 'big day', a Saturday in August, my dad helped me to take the bulging kit-bag and whatever tins of food we could spare to the Scout hut, which was on the gun site near Potter's Barn in Waterloo. We all piled into the waiting furniture van and sat among the tents and big cooking pots, which I later learned were called 'dixies'.
>
> Motorways were still in the future in 1952, so it was an all-day job to get to Ambleside by road, with long delays at Preston and Lancaster. We finally arrived at the farmhouse at the foot of the hill where we were to set up camp, and the furniture van was unable to take us any further, so we trek-carted all the equipment the rest of the way.
>
> Having lived all my twelve years in post-war Litherland, with the bomb site of Bryant & May Ltd Match Makers as our playground, apart from the occasional trip to Southport or New Brighton and days out with the school, I hadn't seen much of the rest of the country.
>
> The Lake District was a whole new wonderful world and an experience I shall never forget. The mountains and lakes were absolutely stunning and although it rained a lot, we didn't care, and spent the ten days wearing shorts, shirts and plimsolls; getting wet and drying out again.
>
> With all the fresh air and exercise, we were ravenous and food never tasted as good as what was cooked on the open fire, and all our drinking water was from a mountain stream.
>
> Things stick in your mind from all those years ago. One thing I remember was going into Ambleside Village and buying bottles of ginger beer, the lids of which we pierced with the 'thing for getting stones out of horses' hooves' on our clasp knives, and when you shook up the bottle, the ginger beer squirted out like a fire extinguisher into your mouth.
>
> I went to many more Scout camps, but nothing matched that first adventure.
>
> The Scouters who took us to Ambleside in 1952 were Jim Shaw, the Group Scoutmaster; Harry Wylie, the Scoutmaster; Tom Mummery, the Assistant Scoutmaster, and Len Bradley. Len did not hold a warrant at the time, but was later to take on the role of GSM and continued to build up the group for very many years. I write this as a tribute to our leaders, who gave up their time to improve our lives.

# 12

# POCKET MONEY

As well as working hard to raise money for his Scout group, Terry Arnot also worked hard to earn some pocket money. He remembers:

> For about two years, 1954-1955, while a pupil at Old Swan Technical School, I was the delivery boy for the Utting Avenue branch of Irwin's grocery store. It was probably the best job I ever had! The 15*s* per-week pay was supplemented by up to 10*s* given by customers when the orders were delivered. These were boxed and carried in a large basket mounted on the front of the 'order bike', which had a small front wheel and a large rear wheel. Manoeuvrability could be difficult when the basket was full of orders or when the weather conditions were bad.
>
> One incident in particular stands out in my memory. Every Saturday morning I had to take Friday's takings to the branch of the Midland Bank, at the bottom of Everton Valley. One Saturday morning in January, the weather was very cold and the roads icy. For some reason, the bike skidded on Walton Breck Road, opposite Liverpool's Football Ground. Both the bike and the rider were sprawled over the road. One of the money bags fell from the basket and the silver coins scattered over the road. In 1954 terms, this was a busy road, and, amid panic, pain and ice, retrieval was difficult but, surprisingly, successful. All the money was duly deposited in the bank! As well as providing spending money, my pay as an order boy also allowed me to open an account at the Post Office Savings Bank – money which I found very useful in later life!

Harold Russell also had a job while still a schoolboy. He was a paper boy, employed by the shop next door to his home. Harold remembers that he got many tips at Christmas, but one special tip stands out in his memory:

> At Easter, I always received half a crown from the priest at St Matthew's, Clubmoor, where I delivered their papers. Half a crown was a lot of money then, and all the more welcome because nobody else tipped at Easter!

Harry Byatt was born in April 1950 in Faulkner Street, Liverpool. He remembers earning pocket money:

> In order to get the money to go to the picture house in Granby Street, we used to go to Great Homer Street or St John's markets to collect empty wooden boxes, to chop them up and sell them as firewood or, if we took about eight empty jam jars, we would have enough. I used to clean houses, deliver coal on foot by the quarter hundredweight, run messages or clean cars. The first car I ever cleaned belonged to the manager of a pub in Faulkner Street.

Mary Allport, living in Bootle, remembers:

> I used to go round the street asking if I could scrub older people's steps, if they could not manage to get down on their knees. They would pay me sixpence. I was very proud of this money. It helped me and our family. By then, I had two brothers and a sister and, being the oldest, everywhere I went, they went. We used to take beer bottles and all kinds of bottles back to the

shop for money. When the rag man came round, we took rags and jam jars to him and we used to get a goldfish in water.

William Duvall also remembers contributing to the family from a young age: 'I delivered milk and papers from the age of twelve, before and after school. We had to pay our way – no Children in Need then and no social workers.'

Some children received pocket money from their parents, older brothers and sisters or other relations. Pauline Bennett says: 'I remember my Mum's three sisters visiting each Monday afternoon and leaving us 3*d* or 6*d* pocket money – money I bet they could ill afford!'

Anne Orme was one of five children, including two sets of twins; she remembers saving pocket money for special occasions:

We would each get sixpence a week pocket money; we would be in a firework club and pay one penny a week into that and one penny a week into a Christmas club. These clubs were at the local paper shop. The remaining fourpence had to last us all week!

Many children did not receive regular pocket money. Sometimes this was because the family income was irregular. Some parents thought that younger children did not need pocket money, as long as they had comics and sweets provided at home. This also meant that parents had more control over what comics were read and sweets were eaten. There were often expectations that some of the money given by uncles, aunts or grandparents, perhaps at birthdays, should be saved.

June Buckley, one of ten children, remembers:

We used to get 2*s* for our birthday present and if we were lucky, threepence for pocket money, but I think this only happened when Dad worked overtime. Other Thursdays, Dad would go to Woolies and get a big bag of sweets, cut up paper to make cornets and fill them with sweets for each of us. We used to go to our aunties' chalets in Sunnyvale in Rhyl, or caravan holidays in Towyn and my dad used to give us a shilling each every day for our spends.

Like Christine McGarry, in West Derby, who earned her pocket money by shopping on Saturday, most children were expected to help in the home in some way, and, for some children, receiving their pocket money depended upon completion of these tasks.

Barry Hignett, born in 1939 in Southport, spent some unhappy years in the Children's Sanatorium in that town, because his mother died in 1941 and his father was in the RAF:

After the war, Dad married again. My two brothers, two sisters and I moved in to a council house with Dad and our new mam. My dad was a bus driver and my mam worked at home. She used to sew leather gloves on a sewing machine as an out-worker. Also, for a couple of years, she used to paint lead soldiers as a part-time job at home. I got sixpence a week pocket money, but I had to earn it. My jobs were chopping wood for kindling to start the coal fire, bringing in the coal and taking out the ashes, taking the wet battery for the radio every week to swap for a fully charged one, and also going to the local shops most days. Sometimes I'd be given a glass pop bottle or a jam jar. I'd take them back to the shop and get tuppence each for them. My sisters' jobs were washing the dishes and helping to wash the clothes and do housework.

Barry helped in another way, now seen as a traditional craft:

We didn't have a Hoover because we had no carpets. The two or three feet of floorboards near the skirting were stained dark brown or covered with lino. The rest of the floor was covered with peg rugs.

The peg rugs were homemade and consisted of old clothes cut into strips about 1in by 4in. The strips of cloth were pushed into holes poked into old hessian sacks. The strips were very close together and they made a good hard-wearing rug. To make larger rugs we just sewed another sack or more together.

Christine Deed found that exam success was a profitable affair:

I don't remember any great fuss being made about the passing of the 11+ exam, although everyone was clearly very pleased at my success because I accumulated quite a lot of gifts of money: 2s from a neighbour, £1 from another, 2s 6d from another, 1s 6d from a cousin. Also a satchel from Grandma, a watch from my godmother and a Conway Stewart pen from Uncle Ernie, the insurance man.

I was also promised piano lessons once all the exams were over and these did indeed materialise. The teacher lived within walking distance in Walton Village and I went there every Friday. Nothing too taxing. No grades because of schoolwork but I did do some theory as well as tunes such as American Patrol and Strauss waltzes. We had an upright piano in the front room and my parents must have been very understanding as I entertained them for far too long.

With 17s 6d of my loot, I went into Liverpool and bought a bag of Butterkist, a doll and clothes, a 'Princess Set', a writing book, a bar of rock, lemonade powder, ribbon and an ounce of wool. And I still had change for … well, no, I seem to have spent the lot!

# 13

# BOOKS AND COMICS

Janet Arnot remembers:

> I used to get the *Dandy* and the *Beano*; later on I had the *Bunty* and the *Judy*. Sometimes, they had 'dress dolls' printed on one page. You pasted the page onto cardboard and cut round the shapes. The dolls were printed with underwear on and the clothes all had shoulder tabs, so that you could hang them on the dolls and play with them.

I had *Rainbow* and *Playbox* when I was quite young; occasionally *Sunny Stories*. Later, I had *Girls' Crystal* on Tuesday, *School Friend* on Wednesday and the *Girl* on Friday. My friends, Gwyneth and Barbara Jones, and I used to pretend to be The Silent Three, who appeared in the *School Friend*. I learned a lot from the *Girl*, which always had a pictorial biography of a famous woman, someone like Mary Slessor, Gladys Aylward or Elizabeth Fry.

The *Girl* magazine also ran stories about girls who were capable of taking charge, like Ray Bailey's Kitty Hawke and her all-girl plane crew. In the wake of the Second World War, when women had fulfilled so many demanding roles, girls wanted to read about their exciting exploits. But the *School Friend's* stories of Princess Anita, who spent her time caring for her subjects, and Jill Crusoe and her friend M'lani, who were castaways on Paradise Island, were equally popular.

The end of paper rationing in 1950 led to amazing choice in comics and magazines. There was always plenty to read in our house. My mother took the *Woman*, the *Woman's Weekly* and the *Home Notes*; my father had *John Bull* magazine, the *Liverpool Echo* and the *Daily Herald*. He also had *The Woodworker* and *Practical Householder*, but I wasn't interested in them! In the *Herald*, there was a cartoon called 'What a Life!' by Gilbert Wilkinson, which I always read, although, as it was often a political comment, I didn't always understand it.

There were plenty of books too. Some of them had been in the family from my mother's childhood or earlier; Victorian books like *The Lamp-Lighter* and *Frankie's Princess*, which were highly improving and extremely sentimental. As I had a cousin, Audrey, who was seven years older than me, I was lucky enough to be given some of her books when she outgrew them. In this way, I read a lot of the Famous Five Books and Enid Blyton's Mystery series, also Malcolm Saville's *Mystery at Witchend*, which was the first of the Lone Pine Adventures. Arthur Ransome's *Swallows and Amazons*, and *Swallowdale*, began my life-long love of the Lake District. As many of these books were part of a long series, I used to save sixpence a week at Baker's newsagent's on County Road, Walton, in order to buy more of them. Fifteen weeks meant, for instance, that I had saved enough for the latest Famous Five book, as these cost 7s 6d.

There were also library books. I joined the library before I was seven years old and had to take a letter from school to say that I could read. The library books were important because, although I received books at Christmas, and always asked for them for my birthday, there were never enough! Quite soon, I was going to Evered Library every Saturday morning with my two friends, Gwyneth and Barbara, who were also avid readers.

Shirley Evans and her brother looked forward to their comics too:

> My favourite comic was *School Friend* and my brother's was the *Beano* or the *Lion*. They were always delivered early in the morning, so our mum would sit on them so we wouldn't read them and be late for school.

Mary Parkin says:

> I loved to read and would get the *Girls' Crystal* and the *School Friend* every week and the annuals at Christmas, as well as the *Rupert Bear annual* every year, too. I loved the stories in the comics and, even though I didn't know what lacrosse was, I was intrigued by the stories of girls at boarding school, which were entirely alien to me and my life. It was great when I went to the library and found an Enid Blyton on the shelf that I hadn't read!

Madeleine Roberts also loved reading: 'I used to love reading the Famous Five books; we didn't have a library in Kirkby, the nearest one was Fazakerley, but I thought it was worth the journey.'

In the 1950s, the notion that working-class children only wanted to read about working-class life, and the more deprived and dysfunctional the better, had not become popular. Nineteen-fifties children were able to read about boarding school life, holidays adventuring in caravans or camping without parents, managing a small boat through the rocks in Kirrin Bay like George in the Famous Five, or sailing to Wild Cat Island and climbing Kanchenjunga – Coniston Old Man – like in *Swallows and Amazons*, without anyone suggesting that it was bad for them to hear about other ways of life, or have their aspirations raised.

Like Shirley Evans and Mary Parkin, Barbara Doran remembers her favourite magazines: 'My mum always bought me two weekly magazines – The *School Friend* and the *Girls' Crystal*. I loved reading them; they were something to look forward to each week.'

The *School Friend* began in 1919; the *Girls' Crystal* in 1935, while the *Girl* magazine did not appear until 1951, when it was introduced as the sister paper to *The Eagle*.

The *Eagle* was first published on 14 April 1950. The creator and editor was Marcus Morris, vicar of St James', Birkdale, who believed that, after the war, there were many fatherless boys who needed good male role models. It was also felt, at the time, that American comic papers were overly violent, amoral and a bad influence. Morris tried to sell the idea of *The Eagle* as a magazine aiming to create an intelligent view of Christianity. He travelled more than once to London on the Sunday midnight train to London Euston from Liverpool Lime Street. Eventually, Hulton Press took on *The Eagle*. The eagle symbol was taken from the top of a brass inkstand that Morris had bought at the vicarage garden party.

Morris had met Frank Hampson at a local school; Hampson created and illustrated *Dan Dare: Pilot of the Future* and also serials such as *The Great Adventurer* (St Paul) and *The Road of Courage* (A life of Christ). Chad Varah, founder of the Samaritans, was one of the early scriptwriters. Frank Bellamy, who took over the Dan Dare stories, also produced many others, including *The Happy Warrior* (The life of Winston Churchill).

Equally as popular as the serious stories were the activities of PC 49, and the legendary detailed cutaways of locomotives, cars, planes and machinery. These have survived in popularity and can now be bought in annual form.

Philip Baker comments: 'I remember my elder brother buying the first issue of *The Eagle*. This was light years away from the *Dandy* and the *Beano* and quickly became required reading for boys.'

The *Lion*, which was a favourite of Shirley Evans' brother, was published from 23 February 1952 and was designed to compete with *The Eagle*. It even had a series called Captain Condor – Space Ship Pilot, a hero intended to rival Dan Dare.

Pauline Bennett had three sisters and a brother:

> We had comics delivered with the daily paper – *Beano, Dandy, Girl* and, I think, *Knockout*. And a boy's comic. I remember buying pop style magazines to read on the bus to school and collecting the pictures of our favourite pop stars – Cliff Richard or Pat Boone.

Chris Brocklehurst remembers that 'some of the comics we read were *Dandy, Beano, Wizard, Rover, Hotspur* and *Adventure*.'

Pat Plunkett remembers American comics and magazines: 'My dad was a merchant seaman, so he used to bring home all sorts of books, magazines and comics, like *Superman, Batman* and all the other DC comics, also True Story and True Romance and others like that.'

The influence of the Cunard Yanks on fashion and music has been well documented, but Pat's comments address the introduction of a different type of cultural influence on people in this country. The *Batman* and *Superman* style of comic were exciting, but did not meet with general approval as reading for young people. The True Confessions, True Romance and True Story type of magazine, which claimed to be based on real experiences, were aimed at grown-up women and dealt in a sensationalised style in the main body of the stories with issues like divorce, tangled relationships and infidelity, which were largely confined to the health or advice columns in magazines like *Woman* and *Woman's Own*, and not even hinted at in the teenage magazines read by Pauline Bennett.

Pat continues:

My friend and I were avid readers and would walk every Saturday to Evered Avenue library. We must have read every book in the junior section – Enid Blyton, Noel Streatfeild and other children's writers. But also books about Perry Mason and Mike Hammer, and also Agatha Christie's novels. I read anything that I could lay my hands on!

The 1950s were the golden age for children's clubs. Some of these grew from the comics or the books that were being read by many children. One of these was The Famous Five Club; the members had badges, which they were encouraged to wear, as Enid Blyton let it be known that

The P.D.S.A. Busy Bees.

This is to Certify that

Pamela Brown

has been enrolled as a P.D.S.A. Busy Bee, and has promised to help the P.D.S.A.

By wearing the Busy Bee Badge constantly "buzzing" about the work of the P.D.S.A.: collecting "honey" for the hive (Woollen Articles of all descriptions, used Foreign, Colonial and English stamps, Silver paper, Tin and Lead foil, Metal Milk bottle tops, rags, bandages, farthings, etc.): being kind to all Animals.

M. E. Dickin, C.B.E.
(Queen Bee.)

Hive Headquarters:
9, Widmore Road,
Bromley, Kent.

*My 'Busy Bee' certificate. Like many other children, I enjoyed helping the People's Dispensary for Sick Animals..*

she would always speak to any child whom she saw wearing the badge. The members of this club were also encouraged to raise money for the Children's Home in Beaconsfield, Buckinghamshire, which was where Enid Blyton lived at Green Hedges, a well-known address to children who read her books.

The Busy Bees was the junior branch of the People's Dispensary for Sick Animals (PDSA); children who were members were encouraged to raise money by collecting silver paper and milk bottle tops to save sick and injured animals. Children wore a badge and received a membership card. The Busy Bees was founded by Maria Dickin CBE; later, Enid Blyton took over her role as Queen Bee. Children received a newsletter with plenty of advice about pet-keeping, information about animals and stories by Enid Blyton about animals.

The Lone Pine Club grew out of Malcolm Saville's series of books about a group of children in Shropshire who had formed their own Lone Pine Club. Children who joined this club received a letter from Malcolm Saville on 'Lone Pine' notepaper, a membership card, a photograph of Malcolm Saville, a Lone Pine badge postcard with a secret code, and a sheet of Lone Pine stamps. These were to stick on the back of letters to friends, who were other Lone Pine Club members. The Lone Pine books were very popular, partly because the first book, *Mystery at Witchend*, involved the club members foiling a group of Nazi spies and saboteurs, which was a typical theme in comics and books in the forties and fifties. But also, some of this group were town children who had moved to the countryside during the war and some were local to the wilds of the Long Mynd; the ages of the children also covered a wide range – from nine-year-old twins, Dickie and Mary, to fifteen-year-old David. There was someone with whom all the readers could identify.

Saville also wrote a series of *Susan and Bill* books, which were based around children who had moved to a newly built estate, One Tree Hill, on the outskirts of the countryside. Children like Anne McCormick, Michael Moran, Dougie Cox, and many others who were having the same experiences, could identify with Susan and Bill.

# 14

# THE CINEMA, TELEVISION AND RADIO

Terry Arnot's pay as a delivery boy allowed him to indulge a favourite pastime of the 1950s – visiting the cinema, or 'going to the pictures' as it was often called.

Terry recalls:

> With the amount of cash earned, a fourteen year old could afford to go to the cinema at least three times a week and became well-versed in the Hollywood glitz and star culture. Cinemas locally were the Ritz, Utting Avenue; the Clubmoor, Townsend Lane; the Regal, Norris Green; the Gaumont, Oakfield Road; the Cabbage Hall, Lower Breck Road and the Victoria, Cherry Lane. Each of these cinemas had programmes that ran from Monday to Wednesday, then a change from Thursday to Saturday and then a one-off programme on a Sunday. One film I remember very well was *Gone with the Wind,* which had a week-long run at the Victoria, Cherry Lane, in about 1955.

Janice Pickthall recalls visiting the cinema with her sister:

> My only sister, Dorothy, was eleven years older than me. She was born in 1936 and had left school before I started at the same school, which was Arnot Street School, off County Road in Walton. Dorothy would take me to 'the pictures' at any of the seven or eight cinemas within a two-mile radius of our home. The Bedford in Bedford Road, Walton, was the nearest.

Like Terry, Janice remembers that films ran from Monday to Wednesday, then from Thursday to Saturday, so that there were always plenty of films to see within an easy distance of home:

> Dorothy and I went to see any musical films that were available – we saw *Calamity Jane, Oklahoma, Carousel, The Student Prince, Seven Brides for Seven Brothers, The Glenn Miller Story, Peter Pan, Tom Thumb, Lady and the Tramp* and lots of others. The National Anthem was always played at the end, but some people would leave their seats and stand at the exit doors before the rush to get out.
>
> I would also go to the Saturday matinee with my friends, where we saw Laurel and Hardy, Abbott and Costello, Charlie Chaplin and cartoons before the weekly serial of *Buck Rogers, Flash Gordon* or *The Lone Ranger.*

Chris Brocklehurst remembers that the children's shows on Saturday were not all at the same time:

> One cinema, the Premier at Green Lane, put on a children's show on a Saturday morning from 11 a.m. to 1.30 p.m., then the Regent on Prescot Road put one on at 2 p.m., so, if you could afford the entrance money for both, you would run up through Old Swan after the morning show to arrive in time for the afternoon one.

Anne McCormick also remembers the Saturday matinees:

> We mostly went to the Coliseum on City Road, when we visited Mum's old home in Walton each week. They used to show cartoons and the big film was mainly about cowboys,

*The Cisco Kid*, *The Lone Ranger* or *Hopalong Cassidy*. Sometimes, we had *Flash Gordon*, which I loved, or *Old Mother Riley*.

Bobbie Binks recalls:

We went every Saturday morning to the Reo in Fazakerley to see Gene Autry, Roy Rogers or Flash Gordon; when the film went off, the shouts of 'Put a shilling in!' were frequent. When we were too young for some films, we used to stand outside one of the many picture houses asking if someone going in to see the film would take you in. Imagine doing that these days!

Peter McGuiness, who was fifteen years old in 1950, remembers becoming more interested in films for grown-ups than in the Saturday matinee:

I was a film fan, but all those under sixteen were hampered in their cinema-going. Films were classified as 'A', where under-sixteens had to be accompanied by an adult and 'U' meant unrestricted. The major chains, Gaumont, Odeon and ABC, interpreted the rules rigidly, so youngsters had no chance of gaining admittance to an 'A' film. To overcome this, we used to stand a few yards from the cinema and ask adult patrons to 'take us in, please?' This was usually successful after a few refusals. Once in the cinema, after your ticket was ripped up, you would not sit by the adult who had taken you in. A drawback for me was that our local cinema, the Carlton, Orrell Park, would not allow in unaccompanied children, even for 'U' films, and the Aintree Palace, which was quite near, made the children sit with any adult who had taken them in – this meant that most adults were reluctant to oblige. The smaller chains tended to turn a blind eye to the rules and, no matter what category of film was showing, you could always get in at the Coliseum, Litherland or the Winter Gardens, Waterloo.

Bert Hamblet was also fifteen in 1950:

I started buying magazines, *The Picturegoer* and the *Picture Show*, in 1950. They both cost threepence. I joined the GPO as a telegraph boy and you would sometimes get a tip of sixpence or a shilling, which meant that you could go to the cinema that night. Once I delivered to a wedding in Boundary Lane and was asked whether I wanted a tip or a kiss from the bride. The bride was no Jane Russell and I remembered there was a good Randolph Scott on at the Cosy in Boaler Street, so I said that I would rather have the tip!

Like Peter McGuiness, Christine McGarry began to prefer adult films and remembers one film that made a big impression:

We went to the Regal in Broadway or the Carlton in Tuebrook. The 'Clubbie' or Clubmoor was not as desirable and was commonly known as the 'fleapit'. I kept away. The only film I can remember with any clarity was *A Summer's Place* with Sandra Dee and Troy Donahue, when I must have been about twelve. An interest in boys was starting and this love story really affected me.

Barbara Doran recalls:

Visits to the cinema were known as 'going to the pictures' – there was the Gaumont and the Beresford in Park Road or the Mayfair and the Rivoli in Aigburth Road. I remember the organ being played in the intervals and that the Mayfair organ always used to change colour!

Mary Parkin lived in Roscommon Street:

> We had two cinemas in Rossy – the Tivoli, known as the Tivvy, near the top of the street, which had wooden seating and the Roscommon, known as the Rossy, near the bottom of the street, which had red plush seats. Nearly every Saturday morning, I would go to the matinee at the Tivvy with my friends, but, before we joined the queue, we would go to the fruit shop opposite and get a bag of 'fades', which was fruit which wasn't quite at its best, to take into 'the pictures'. The Tivvy always smelt of 'wee', as a lot of the children didn't quite make it to the toilet and just let nature take its course, where they sat! We loved it though and there was always a main feature and a second feature to see. There was always an usherette with a torch who constantly paraded around to keep order.
>
> The Rossy was the superior cinema, if you could call it that, and I would often go with my nana to keep her compan,y as she was widowed when I was about nine or ten years old.

Eileen Pritchard remembers that:

> My Mum loved going to the cinema and went out on her own on Monday and Thursday evenings to any of the local cinemas – the Princess, the Reo, the Astoria, the Queens, the Bedford, the Carlton, the Commodore, the Walton Vale. Dad used to stay at home to look after me; I used to sit on the top of the stairs and listen to the radio downstairs as Dad used to have it on very loud as he was hard of hearing; he often caught me and ticked me off.
>
> Saturday afternoon matinees were fantastic. We paid about sixpence and yelled our way through the picture, standing up and cheering when the goodies – the cavalry – arrived at the crucial moment to save everyone. Quite often fights would break out amongst the kids – the staff had a difficult time controlling everyone.
>
> Saturday nights were a family event; we lived in the same street as the Princess Cinema and, no matter what the programme was, we went as a family. I was often bored stiff and wriggled and yawned throughout the film – I was frequently told off!

William Duvall remembers visiting the cinema:

> Saturday afternoon was pictures time – the Tunnel in Tunnel Road, later called the Avenue, I think, or the one on Smithdown Road, which was a bit more upmarket than the Tunnel, so not as many fights. Zorro was the hero of the day, or Errol Flynn. The Tunnel was threepence; the other was sixpence or thereabouts, but it was all good fun for young boys.

William also remembers when his granddad appeared on television:

> There was a programme called *People and Places* hosted by Bill Grundy. It was on TV about 1955 to 1965. My granddad was on it in 1959; it caused quite a stir in our street. We were one of the two houses with a TV in those days. My cousin, Jim, had to take Granddad to the Granada studios in Manchester. It was the other side of the world to them; anyway, all the street, or so it seemed, crammed into our house to see this 'celebrity'. The topic was vandalism – when Granddad sold soap powder outside the wash house, he looked after the housewives' old prams on which they carried their washing. Otherwise kids, us included, would nick them and make what we called steeries or steering carts (like go-carts) using the wheels. You needed two sets of wheels, a plank of wood and an old box and you were off. Like everything in those days, even vandalism was innocent.

Liz Egerton, born in 1955, remembers programmes for younger children with affection: 'I remember watching *Watch with Mother*, *The Wooden Tops* and *Andy Pandy* on a rediffusion set.'

*Watch with Mother* was a cycle of children's programmes created by Freda Lingstrom and broadcast by BBC television from 1952. It was the first BBC television programme specifically aimed at pre-school children, like its radio equivalent *Listen with Mother*. The best-remembered programmes were *Picture Book* on Mondays from 1955, *Andy Pandy* on Tuesdays from 1950, *The Flowerpot Men* on Wednesdays from 1952, *Rag, Tag and Bobtail* on Thursdays from 1953 and *The Woodentops* on Fridays from 1955 with 'the very biggest spotty dog you ever did see!'

Audrey Atterbury, a puppeteer, brought *Andy Pandy* to *Watch with Mother* and it has been said that the lovable little boy puppet was based on her son, Paul, who is well known as an expert on *The Antiques Roadshow*. Andy Pandy was a solo performer in the early programmes, but was later joined by Teddy and a rag doll, Looby Loo.

*Muffin the Mule*, another puppet show, was broadcast from 1946 and was aimed at children of all ages.

Mary Parkin remembers Muffin:

I loved watching *Whirligig* and *Muffin the Mule*, whose strings could be seen quite clearly. Annette Mills wore an evening dress and sat at a grand piano as she spoke to the puppet. All the announcers wore evening dress and seemed so posh!

Margaret Dunford remembers some favourite programmes:

I think we got a telly when I was about eight. We sat all day watching the Test Card and then *Billy Bean* came on with his Funny Machine and also *Muffin the Mule*. I think The *Grove Family* were on in the fifties too.

Anne Orme comments: 'My grandma, who lived next door, must have been well-off as she was one of the first people we knew who had a television. We would all go in to watch *The Grove Family*.'

Christine McGarry recalls watching television with the family:

Television was watched in short spells. We had three generations vying for it and my granddad loved *The Brains Trust* – very highbrow and too intellectual for me. I loved *Rawhide, The Cisco Kid, Bonanza* and one of the earliest soaps called *The Grove Family*. I can remember my grandma being incensed by the dancing girls on Sunday Night at the London Palladium. She thought their skimpy clothes highly indecent!

Christine, Anne and Margaret all remember *The Grove Family,* which was a favourite in our house too.

*The Grove Family* was the first 'soap' for adults, although that term was not yet used in this country to describe television programmes. *The Groves* were named after the BBC's Lime Grove Studio. The serial began on Friday, 2 April 1954, and by the end of that year about 9 million people were following the life of this average family. People even wrote to get estimates from the father, Bob Grove, who was a builder. The elder son is seen wearing an old flying jacket, as many of the young male audience would have been wearing old items of uniform from the war or National Service, and both he and his father smoke in almost every scene. The younger son, Lennie, was played by Christopher Beeny, who later became famous as Edward, the footman in *Upstairs Downstairs.*

Another popular family serial, *The Appleyards*, was transmitted fortnightly from 1952 on Thursdays, between 4.30 p.m. and 5 p.m. on children's television, but the repeat performance on Sunday teatime was watched with enjoyment by many adults. Like *The Groves*, it dealt with everyday situations that the viewers would recognise: the lonely neighbour who was asked to

Christmas dinner, the rivalries caused by a local election and the decision, taken very seriously, by the younger daughter as to whether or not she should be confirmed.

There was no sensationalism in these programmes and, far from indulging in criminal activity, the first episode of *The Grove Family*, written by Michael and Roland Pertwee and entitled 'Prevention and Cure', deals with home security. A great deal of advice about securing doors and windows was included in the dialogue. The episode concludes with this advice foiling an opportunist burglar.

Commercial television began on 9 September 1955, and the first advertisement, for Gibbs SR toothpaste, was shown at 8.20 p.m. The Television Act of 1954 had made the formation of the Independent Television Authority possible, but the government had made it clear that advertising and programmes were to be clearly separated. This was in contrast to some programmes in the United States, where product placement by programme sponsors could be intrusive.

Before television ownership became widespread, the radio supplied entertainment and many of the radio shows were very popular.

The British Broadcasting Corporation (BBC) commanded great respect. It had played an important role during the war years in maintaining morale, not only by broadcasting the news and Winston Churchill's rousing speeches, but also in its hints for coping with rationing and offering gardening tips and, with comedy and light entertainment, keeping people cheerful. The BBC was an important part of most people's lives.

There were three main BBC radio stations. The Light Programme with popular music, variety shows, comedy and drama; the Home Service also broadcast general entertainment and it was the main channel for news, features and regional programmes. The Third Programme was recognised as 'highbrow' and, in the 1950s, was broadcast only in the evenings. It featured classical music, serious and experimental drama, poetry readings and talks on suitably scientific or philosophical topics. Most of the population rarely bothered with it.

Some of the lighter entertainment programmes included *Take It From Here*, written by Frank Muir and Denis Norden and starring Jimmy Edwards, Dick Bentley and Joy Nichols; later June Whitfield and Alma Cogan joined the cast. *Take It From Here* began in 1948 and continued throughout the 1950s. It introduced the popular feature The Glums, featuring a long-running engagement between Ron Glum and his fiancée, Eth. It struck a chord with listeners because lengthy engagements were quite usual in the 1950s. The shortage of housing in the aftermath of the Blitz meant that most couples had to wait to find affordable housing. The alternative was to live with other members of the family and one consequence of this situation was that many children of the fifties grew up in extended families.

Other popular programmes included *Family Favourites*, which had begun during the war as *Forces Favourites*. It was a request programme linking families with servicemen and women. It was broadcast at Sunday lunchtime and, for many people, its signature tune 'With a Song in my Heart' is inextricably linked with thoughts of a roast dinner and milk pudding or apple pie. The introduction: 'The time in Britain is twelve noon, in Germany it's one o'clock, but home and away, it's time for Two-Way Family Favourites' was very familiar and, today, very nostalgic.

Families sat down together in the evening to listen to the radio, often with other activities going on around them: eating, knitting, doing a jigsaw, the football pools or a crossword puzzle. Daytime programme planners recognised that people would be busy working, so *Worker's Playtime* and *Music While You Work* were lively and cheerful. Other favourite programmes were *Woman's Hour, Listen with Mother, Children's Hour, Life with the Lyons, Journey into Space, Mrs Dale's Diary, The Adventures of PC 49, Much Binding in the Marsh, Ray's a Laugh* with comedian Ted Ray, *The Navy Lark* and *Meet the Huggetts*, featuring the respectable salt-of-the-earth Huggett family. Jack Warner and Kathleen Harrison played Joe and Ethel Huggett on the radio and in several successful films, of which the best known is *Holiday Camp*.

Shelagh Nugent remembers the old-fashioned type of radio:

> Our wireless was powered by a huge battery. When the battery ran out, it had to be carted to the hardware shop in an old shopping bag and exchanged for a fresh one. You had to be careful not to spill the acid.

Mary Parkin recalls the mysteries of the workings of the 'wireless':

> We often listened to the wireless and I remember the accumulator man coming on Saturdays to change the accumulator in the wireless. I didn't know much about it except that there was something to do with acid! As we didn't have electricity at that time, we had to have the battery topped up each week.
>
> I listened to *Uncle Mac* and loved *Sparky*, I'm a Pink Toothbrush, You're a Blue Toothbrush by Max Bygraves, and the songs Danny Kaye used to sing.

Danny Kaye, born David Daniel Kaminsky in 1913, was an extremely successful American actor, dancer, singer and comedian, well known for comic songs, some of which came from the film *Hans Christian Andersen*. The film was released in 1952, billed as Samuel Goldwyn's Screen Masterpiece and featuring songs like The Ugly Duckling, Wonderful Copenhagen, The Inch Worm and Thumbelina, which became extremely popular with all age groups.

Mary continues:

> We listened to *Journey into Space, A Life of Bliss, Life with the Lyons, The Navy Lark, Take It From Here, Take Your Pick* and, of course, *Educating Archie*, where a ventriloquist performed on the wireless! We would spend hours, as a family, listening to the wireless. Mum listened to *Woman's Hour* and *Mrs Dale's Diary*, which were daytime programmes.

Shirley Evans also remembers cosy evenings at home:

> In the evening I would sit on the settee with Mum and Dad either reading or listening to the radio. Some of our radio favourites were *Dick Barton – Special Agent* and *Take It From Here*. The radio was quite old and I can remember carrying the accumulators to the local shop to be re-charged. We also had gas lights so when the mantle went I used to go to the local shop for a new one. I remember having to be very careful carrying them as they were very fragile.

Janet Arnot also remembers listening to the radio:

> Dad rigged up a speaker from the wireless, which meant that my sister and I could listen to the radio upstairs or in bed, but my parents had control over what we were listening to. I really liked the wooden speaker because it had a fretwork design on the front with red and gold brocade material behind it.

Janice Pickthall, born in 1947, remembers:

> We didn't have a television until I was nine or ten and it was a 14in screen Bush model bought from Banners on County Road. Prior to this, I remember tuning in to Radio Luxembourg on the wireless on a Sunday night to listen to *Take Your Pick*, which was my mother's favourite. We had to listen intently as the sound always faded at the crucial moment when the box was opened and the contestant would find out what they had won. Sometimes we never knew!

*Take Your Pick* was a very popular game show that appeared on Radio Luxembourg in the early 1950s and later transferred to television, when ITV began in 1955. Contestants had to survive the 'Yes–No Interlude' when they were required to answer a rapid stream of questions without using the words Yes or No. They then chose a numbered key to a box, which they were tempted to 'sell' to the Quiz Inquisitor, Michael Miles. Janice refers to the moment when they would finally open the box to reveal their prize. The prizes could be a holiday or a new luxury item, such as a washing machine, but they could also be a booby prize, like a box of matches or a mousetrap.

Anne McCormick also remembers Radio Luxembourg:

My sister and I joined the *Ovaltineys* who used to broadcast on Radio Luxembourg as I recall. Each week we would tune in and you would be given a coded message over the airways. You then had to refer to your membership info and use the code to interpret the message. We thought we were very clever working this out.

Margaret Gillson was another Ovaltiney: 'I used to listen to the Ovaltineys and remember entering a competition and winning a box of mixed bars of Cadbury's chocolate, which was really something in those days!'

The *Ovaltineys* originated in the 1930s, but they were revived in 1952 and many children became Ovaltineys, while many more listened regularly. Radio Luxembourg was broadcast on 208 MW. It began broadcasting from Luxembourg in 1948 and advertised various products, as the very successful *Ovaltineys* demonstrated. One of its most well-known programme sponsors was Horace Batchelor, who promoted a winning football pools formula and his address became famous as Keynsham – spelt K-E-Y-N-S-H-A-M – Bristol, with thousands of listeners.

Radio Luxembourg was the only station broadcasting non-stop popular music and became increasingly the station for young people, or teenagers, as they became known in the 1950s. Radio Luxembourg satisfied their desire for plenty of their own sort of music, which, as the decade progressed, was not the choice of their parents. It also continued to increase its audience as young people began to own transistor radios, or trannies, and was the forerunner of the pirate radio stations which, paradoxically, brought about a decrease in its popularity.

# 15

# SPORT AND GAMES

There was plenty of opportunity in the 1950s for children and teenagers to get involved in sport and games at various levels. School sport was worthwhile and very competitive and there were also many clubs that people could join for reasonable fees.

Christine Deed remembers arriving at the Queen Mary High School in Long Lane, Aintree, which had large playing fields, tennis courts, netball courts and a well-equipped gym, to sit the scholarship exam:

> As we entered the grounds, I spotted the netball courts and pitifully sought reassurance from Mum that they wouldn't make me play games if I passed. Not wanting to upset me before the exam she, of course, lied through her teeth. I thought of her when I eventually ended up on freezing winter days running up and down the hockey pitch.

Although not all children welcomed the opportunity for sport that schools offered, there were many young people who enjoyed the experience of taking part.

Moira Kennedy attended St Michael's RC School: 'I played all the sports, being in the hockey and netball teams and I loved swimming at Margaret Street or Lister Drive baths. In summer, we loved going to New Brighton open-air pool.'

Some also welcomed the opportunities for leadership that existed. Harold Russell attended Roscoe Garsfield Secondary Modern School:

*Roscoe Garsfield football team, 1952. Harold Russell is on the far left in the front row.*

I played cricket and football for the fourth year teams in 1952 and, in my last year, was lucky enough to be picked to play football for Liverpool Schoolboys.

The school comprised four houses, named after historic Liverpool dignitaries: Roscoe, Gladstone, Rathbone and Derby. The House Colour for Derby was yellow. I was proud to be captain of Derby House which won the House Cup twice during my time as captain, never having won the cup before then.

Harold also remembers his interest, during the mid-1950s, in cycling and cycle racing:

I became a member of the Mersey Roads Cycling Club. At that time, the Mersey Roads Club was well known in the cycling world with a few members being national champions in twenty-five and fifty mile time trials. I rode in both road races and time trials, and travelled as far as Derby to compete in time trials and Cheshire to compete in road races. The club was one of only two clubs in the country to organise and stage an annual twenty-four hour time trial. As stewards for this event, we would have to camp out at strategic places to guide riders on the correct course during the night.

Peter McGuiness remembers:

There was a tremendous enthusiasm for sport throughout the whole of society, both as watchers and performers. I had no real aptitude for most sports, but I did participate in cycling. I was one of many Liverpool cyclists who, every Sunday, rode to the Pier Head, went over on the Woodside ferry and cycled to North Wales, via Chester or Queensferry. I was purely a tourist and did not join a club, merely went out with my school friends. Between 5 p.m. and 8 p.m., on Sundays in the summer, the New Chester Road was filled with cyclists heading for the Woodside ferry and there was a great feeling of fellowship when talking to other cyclists about where they had been or what they thought of new equipment on the market.

On my first Sunday out in North Wales on my bike, although I was wearing shorts, my mother insisted that I wore a collar and tie, because it was Sunday and it was common to be seen without a tie.

Throughout the winter, my friends and I went every Saturday to see either Everton or Liverpool. The entrance fee was just nine old pence (about 4p), so there were seldom problems with money. Neither of our local teams were very successful during this period, but these were really enjoyable afternoons out; in effect, they were social occasions. We always had a good time on Saturday afternoons although, of course, it was better if our team won. I cannot recall any trouble with spectators; certainly, opposing fans were not segregated. There was good-natured banter and occasional swearing, but no obscene chanting or violent behaviour.

The players were part of the local community. They often travelled to the match on the same bus as we did. Sometimes they would be in the same cinema queue as we were on Saturday night. In those days, players and spectators were all part of the same community.

Ken Lloyd, like many other children, remembers the serious business of the 'pools' coupon:

My father used to fill out the Vernons football pools each week and quite often I used to help him pick matches which I thought would end in a draw. He usually did perms (permutations), which were, say, 3 columns of 4 matches and 4 columns of 4 matches (separated by a sloped line) and underneath you wrote 'perm any 3 from 4 = 12 lines at 1d'. The maximum was 24 points so you tried to pick 8 matches which would end in a draw (3 points). A home win was 1 point and an away win was 2 points. The prize for 24 points was £75,000, which would be shared if there was more than one winner. He would post them each week, complete with a postal order to the value of the bet. In the summer he did similar, but it was the Australian matches.

David Russell was a pupil at St Margaret's High School, Anfield (SMA), now situated in Aigburth and, thus, able to retain its initials and the Essemay Old Boys title. David was a keen cross-country runner:

During the winter we would be encouraged to go cross-country running. The playing fields of SMA were at Dwerryhouse Lane, where we went one half-day a week and were given tickets – 3*d*, 4*d* etc. – to get the bus home.

To play football, you had to be a potentially good player who could play for the school. I never achieved this greatness at football, unlike my brother who played for Liverpool Schoolboys. However, I quite liked the relative solitude of cross-country running.

We had two courses from Dwerryhouse Lane; one took us along Dwerryhouse to the Western Approaches pub – I never did stop for a quick one – down Storrington Avenue to Croxteth Hall Lane and, eventually, back to the playing fields. The other course was much more pleasant, running down Oak Lane to Croxteth Hall Lane, through Croxteth Hall Park to St Mary's Church in West Derby Village and then back to Dwerryhouse Lane via Meadow Lane.

I became quite good, although I always kept something in reserve to make sure I got back! In retrospect, it's a shame really, because if I could have let go more and gone flat out, perhaps I could have beaten Bellard and Coleman, my teammates, and done better when the medals and cups were given out! However, I did get a medal for our team performance at the Pembroke Harriers Relay.

My best memory was going by minibus to a race at Bolton Harriers; we were running late and the roads were very busy. I don't know how it happened but we ended up with a police escort to the sports ground. We didn't win but what an entrance!

Being a member of the school cross country team, you were awarded Colours in the fifth year. Colours meant that you replaced your blazer badge, which was black and white, for a coloured badge which you wore with pride! The problem came in the Lower 6th, when I was made a Prefect. This was yet another badge and quite impressive – however, the colours won the day and, whilst I enjoyed being a Prefect, I still sported my Colours blazer badge!

# 16

# GOING TO WORK

In 1944, the school-leaving age had been raised to fifteen. Grammar school children stayed at school until at least age sixteen, possibly eighteen, and some went on to university or college. The years when children left school and went to work at fourteen were at an end. But even though starting work for most people in the 1950s began at fifteen or sixteen years of age, this did not signal financial independence. Realistic contributions to the family budget were expected, and very few young people had much disposable income. The youth club was not just for schoolchildren; it was an important part of many people's teenage social lives, because it was affordable.

Children were still not seen as independent until they were twenty-one years old. Until then, they were answerable to their parents, who expected to set rules about general behaviour. The bestowal of 'the key of the door' at twenty-one was not necessarily strictly maintained, for practical reasons. But it did have the symbolism of pointing out that the 'comings and goings' of young people were under supervision!

Chris Brocklehurst had older brothers, but he chose a different career path from them:

As some of my brothers became eighteen years old, they went into the army. I left school at fifteen and my first job was in Crawford's Biscuit Works in Binns Road. All wages were given to my mum – even my dad's! I was only at Crawford's for four months when I left to go into the Merchant Navy for the next ten years. My life taught me to work for what you wanted and not to rely on others and to save up for what you want.

Cliff Duncan remembers his first job:

I took a job as a cinema projectionist to help keep the wolf from the door. I was desperate to earn money to help my family. The job was poorly paid and the hours were long and unsociable. We worked from 10 a.m. to 11 p.m. daily with one day off and a Sunday evening. My cinema was the Gaumont in Anfield, near to Liverpool's football ground. I was employed by the Cinema Management Association, which was part of the Rank Organisation.

I enjoyed the work and did my best. They sent me on two courses. One was at the Hippodrome in Liverpool and the other was at the Odeon, Swiss Cottage, in London, which I also enjoyed, while privately deciding that this was not a career that I wished to follow.

Enid Johnston, *née* Mole, had attended St Hilda's School for Girls:

When I left school I went to work in the offices of Bryant & May Ltd Match Makers in Speke Road, Garston. My job was receptionist/switchboard/typist. I had training as a shorthand typist, but there was no vacancy for one at that time. It was a lovely office building, set apart from the factory. It had high old-fashioned desks for the clerks, like something out of a Dickens book. I used to like being asked to go into the factory, which was incredibly noisy, but it was fascinating to see how the matches were made. Bryant & May had super dances in the works canteen and there were tennis courts. Three of us girls used to support the cricket team and go to their away matches and make tea for the teams at home games.

Agnes Jones remembers her first job:

It was as a typist in a law stationery firm. We had to walk up rickety wooden stairs and three of us were in a postage-stamp size room with the boss in a cubby-hole off it. We typed legal documents on old-fashioned typewriters and were allowed very few erasures. The boss would hold the documents up to the light to see if there was a mark on the paper from the eraser. Sometimes we had to copy old Wills. The originals of these documents were hand-written on old parchment and were picked up from Liverpool City Council. These had to be taken back every night as they were irreplaceable. I was the messenger girl and always had a fear of dropping one of these Wills down the drain gratings in the gutter!

Milk was short and had to be scalded so it could be used again for morning tea next day. Of course, I also had to brew the tea. One day, I scalded the milk and poured it into a glass bottle. There was glass and milk all over the floor!

Doreen Stock completed a two-year tailoring course at the Mabel Fletcher Technical College in Wavertree:

We were all placed with tailors in the city, of which there were many. My job was with a bespoke ladies' tailor, Mr Kalinsky, at No. 114 Bold Street – the Bond Street of the North – it was a hive of activity with a furrier on the first floor and Maggs Antiques on the ground floor. I enjoyed working there for nearly two years. When Mr Kalinsky retired, I began straightaway as a cutter at Nanette's on County Road in Walton. Finding another job wasn't a problem then! Nanette's had a large workroom above the shop with many machinists. There were two cutting rooms, a large room with tables and chairs to eat our lunch and an office. Every few weeks, a special wedding display was made for the London Road branch and Nanette's also had fashion shows in the concert room at St George's Hall.

Barbara Doran, born in 1940, started work in 1955 and lived in the Dingle:

I went to work as a printer and bookbinder at Sutton's. There I made school exercise books. I was paid, as an apprentice, £1 6s 5d per week. The hours were quite long for a fifteen year old – 8 a.m. to 5.15 p.m. with only half an hour for lunch. If you were late more than three times, you were sacked on the spot.

I used to travel to work on the Overhead Railway from Dingle station to James Street station. There were two classes of carriage. First class had plush material seats, while the lower-class carriage had plywood seats that were very uncomfortable. I never ever sat in first class; it was too expensive.

*A ticket for the Overhead Railway.*

The Liverpool Overhead Railway was opened on 4 February 1893 by the prime minister, Lord Salisbury. It was the first electric elevated rail system in the world and one of the first with automatic signalling. It was also the fourth metropolitan railway system in the world, after the London underground and elevated railways in New York and Chicago.

It was unique in that the track bed was formed of iron sheeting to prevent litter falling through the open rails onto the streets below, which was a problem with New York's elevated railway. This feature also led to its affectionate nickname, the Dockers' Umbrella, since it was possible to walk its length from dock to dock in shelter from rain or snow.

In the early twentieth century, the line was linked with the Lancashire & Yorkshire Railway, making a number of connections possible, notably a link with Aintree station and, thus, the racecourse.

Changes in the way that business was conducted, particularly the use of the telephone, meant that fewer messengers were constantly using the line. But its potential as a tourist attraction had been noted. There was a poster advertising the Overhead Railway with an attractive vista of the ships and docks and the words: 'A round trip of thirteen miles of the Best Way to see the Finest Docks in the World and the Great Ocean Liners'. Another poster showed the open-air swimming pool in Southport, pointing out that it was possible to travel daily to Southport by the Liverpool Overhead Railway.

By the mid-1950s, the Overhead Railway was in desperate need of maintenance work. Neither the Liverpool Corporation nor the Mersey Docks and Harbour Board were willing to support the necessary works financially. In 1957, the Overhead Railway was demolished.

At the time, with great foresight, Mr H. Maxwell Roston, the General Manager of the Liverpool Overhead Railway, said:

> The time will come when Merseysiders must rue the day when they permitted the City Fathers to throttle the lifeblood of this unique undertaking and in addition to scrap the last vestige of their remarkably efficient tramway system.

Today, the tourist industry in Liverpool would find the Overhead Railway a huge asset.

Harold Russell's first job involved travelling on the Overhead Railway:

> I left school in June 1953 with no qualifications and no job. I always wanted to work in a ship-owner's office but, unfortunately, when I left school there were no vacancies in any of the Liverpool Ship-owners' offices and I signed on at the Liverpool Youth Employment Office in Sir Thomas Street. Having explained what sort of work I wanted, I was interviewed and got the job at Scruttons and Co. Ltd, opposite the Queen Victoria Monument.
>
> In those days, the Monument was probably the only building standing on that side of the road and all one side of Lord Street was flat due to the bombing during the war. This area was covered with cinders and, every lunchtime, after eating my homemade sandwiches at my desk, I would meet up with an old school friend and play football on the cinder pitch.
>
> There was always a game at lunchtime, with teams being up to fifteen or twenty a side! We would go 'pudding or beef', and one of the players would choose and my friend and I would play one on each side. We would end up filthy after an hour playing on the cinders and I would have to go into the gent's at the office to get washed before I could start work after lunch.

Like Harold and his friends, Pat Plunkett went to work while still happy to join in street games: 'I left school in 1952, aged fifteen, but at that age I was still playing out in the street with my friends, games like rounders, skipping or hide-and-seek.'

But young people were expected to be responsible and hard-working in the workplace, while still being relatively unsophisticated in many ways.

Harold continues:

> Scruttons were Stevedores and Master Porters were employing dock workers to load and discharge ships. My job, as office boy, was to take letters to the ship-owners' offices in the city and then take shipping notes to the various docks where the ships were being discharged or loaded. This meant travelling on the Liverpool Overhead Railway to SW3 Canada Dock and Harrington Dock – these docks being at one end of the Liverpool Docks from the other.

After doing other jobs within Scruttons, like drawing-up ships' stowage plans from the Mate's boat notes, I was becoming known at the various ship owners' offices and my wish to work in one of them came true.

On one of my many visits to MacAndrews and Co. Ltd, part of the Andrew Weir Group, I was asked if I would like to work with them, as a vacancy had been made by one of the eighteen year olds being called up for National Service. I said 'Yes', but was told that I would have to apply in writing, which I did. I was successful and got the job, but now came my dilemma.

Mr Sharrock, the manager of MacAndrews, had lunch with Mr Pullen, my manager at Scruttons, every day and I did not like the idea of Mr Sharrock telling Mr Pullen before I handed in my resignation. Mr Sharrock eased the situation for me. He would mention my intended move but wait for Mr Pullen to employ a suitable replacement before I started work with MacAndrews. This was done and all Mr Pullen said to me was, 'I believe you are leaving us.' He wished me all the best and I never tendered my resignation letter.

It is intriguing to wonder whether these two managers arranged the whole move between them over lunch, knowing of Harold's ambition. They were justified, if so, since, after working his way up through various roles within the company, finally, Harold became manager of the Liverpool end of the whole company.

Harold remembers the social aspects of working for a large company:

I started work as a junior office clerk at McAndrews on 19 July 1954 and soon became friends with all the staff and, throughout those years, we were a family and it was said that 'we worked for each other, not the company'. We socialised in the evenings; we had teams in the Liverpool shipping staff's table tennis and football leagues, both eleven and five-a-side. We also had MacAndrews' ten pin bowling team, called 'The Avengers', playing in the league at the Tuebrook Bowl.

Although Harold found his first job in an office through his own efforts, with a little help from the Youth Employment Service, the guidance he had received from his school had related only to factory work. As he explains:

School visits to proposed places of work were major events during my last year; these visits were categorised by the pupils on where you got the best lunch, not where you would like to work. The two top visits were British Steel at Queensferry and Cronton Colliery at Widnes. Both these companies put on a very good meal for lunch but not many of us liked the idea of working at a coal mine or working on the line at a very hot steel mill. Jacob's biscuit factory, where we got a bag of broken biscuits, and Ogden's cigarette factory were other visits we made during my last school year.

Peter McGuiness remembers very little information being available:

Career guidance at school was very limited. There were pamphlets available in the library and the odd careers talk from a representative of a particular trade, profession or company. There were no careers evenings at school to which parents were invited, nor do I remember ever speaking to a careers teacher. The major driving force seemed to be parents. I often heard the expression, 'My dad can get me into his firm', sometimes with a proviso about a particular qualification, but, in some companies in those days there seemed to be a strong family tradition, almost amounting to an hereditary principle.

*Harold Russell, centre, with colleagues at a company dinner in London. In the 1950s, young people attended and enjoyed formal events like this dinner dance. It was a part of joining the adult world.*

Peter remembers that by the final year at school:

> My friends were quite realistic at this stage. Gone were the dreams of being footballers, film stars or Spitfire pilots. There were more down-to-earth plans.
>
> Lots of girls wanted to be air hostesses. It had a glamorous appeal, an attractive uniform and the prospect of travel to exotic locations. This was no pipe-dream; two of my contemporaries obtained employment with airlines, but as they both gave the job up after a relatively short period, it may not have been such a desirable occupation after all!

In the 1950s, girls had much more independence than had been usual before the war and many saw the job of air hostess as Peter describes it – glamorous and sophisticated. The advertisements of many airlines showed the air hostesses as one of their major assets, combining attraction with care and kindness to the traveller. In reality, as today, it was a very tiring and demanding job and the opportunities to see the various destinations to which they travelled were probably more limited than they had anticipated.

# 17

# NATIONAL SERVICE

In 1948, peacetime conscription was formalised so that from 1 January 1949, healthy males aged 17–21 were expected to serve in the Armed Forces for eighteen months. They were exempt if in mining, farming or the Merchant Navy. Many young men from Liverpool preferred the Merchant Navy as a more adventurous option, which they thought also offered more freedom. In 1950, because of Britain's involvement in the Korean War, the period of National Service was extended to two years. In some ways, National Service could be seen as an end to childhood, but, for many boys, it extended the period of freedom from adult responsibilities of home, wife and children.

Harold Russell remembers the leaving of Liverpool:

On 9 May 1957, my dad took me to Lime Street station in his company van. I was off to the Royal Army Ordnance Corps (RAOC) Hilsea Barracks, Portsmouth. It was my first time travelling on my own. Saying goodbye, I thought I would not see Mum, Dad or my brother for two years. Bearing in mind that I had been issued with rail tickets and, therefore, I just had to show them to the ticket collectors, I did not speak to a soul until we got to just outside of Portsmouth. Then I realised that boys my age on the train were going to the same place as me and conversations started to flow.

In our instructions, we had been given a time window in which to report. We arrived just after midday. An army lorry, with the canvas cover off, was waiting at the station and we were escorted to the lorry by two corporals; one was the driver and one was riding shotgun. We piled on the lorry, all in civvies, with our little cases and we were off to Hilsea Barracks via the town centre. I remember it was a very sunny day and the lads started to wolf-whistle at all the girls in Portsmouth as we passed on our way to the barracks.

When we arrived, the barracks gates appeared to be massive as they shut behind us, and, as they shut, it seemed that the weather changed and it started to rain. The first bit of kit we were issued, due to this downpour, was a groundsheet/cape. We stood on the square, still in civvies with our little cases, with the capes draped around us, getting soaked. Then the big gates opened and in drove a taxi. The taxi did a complete circle around the square, stopped, and four Geordies rolled out, drunk as lords! This, of course, made us laugh until we were put in our place by corporals bawling at us, 'Stop laughing, please, you are in the army now!' or something like that! The Geordies had, no doubt, been given the same window as us to arrive, but decided to leave it to the last minute! They were slung into the guardroom cells until the next morning.

After ten weeks, I was sent to Aldershot to train as a Store Keeper First Class. Despite having been in the Liverpool schoolboys football team and being a member of the Mersey Roads Cycling Club, I did not apply for the army teams because they did not go abroad – and that was what I wanted. In the event, I was sent to Beeston Barracks near Nottingham, instead of Cyprus, Germany, Malaya or anywhere the British Army were at the time. That was the end of one ambition!

Many things that happened seem funny now, but, at the time, one did not think that they were funny. I remember being in a Gala Sports Day in a field not far from the camp; lots of tents were pitched around the ground for the various activities, like contestants signing in for events, changing facilities and the like. Having finished running in our events, four or five of us went to the back of these tents, lay down in the sun and fell asleep. When I woke up, all the tents had gone. My so-called friends had left me and I was on my own in running gear. I ran back to camp and past the guardroom as if I were the last runner in the marathon!

As I had played the drums in the Scouts, I applied to the bandmaster to join the band and I was accepted. This meant the colour of my webbing had to be changed to white, but, best of all, no guard duties and irregular work practices, due to band practice. A few months before this, I had been promoted to Lance Corporal and, sometimes, an acting unpaid unwanted Corporal. This meant that I was the second highest rank in the band; the Drum Major being a Sergeant. During my last six months of National Service, many camps were closing down all over the country and each camp closure meant a parade and march past with a Field Marshall or General taking the salute and an army band present. We had our own single-decker bus that took us all over the country closing down camps. Our kit was in good order so little maintenance was needed to keep it up to scratch and, because the Generals were present, the food was always good. Best of all, we had plenty of spare time to go into the local towns each night.

We had a full inspection every month when a Field Marshall or General came to inspect the camp and the troops. On one of these occasions the Drum Major was on leave so I was in charge of the band. On these occasions the band played in one corner of the square while the battalion marched up and down and the Drum Major did not play an instrument or carry the mace. Then the Regimental Sergeant Major marched up to the band and me. He wanted the band to fall in, in front of the platoon, and take the battalion on a march through the camp, including the married quarters, where I had never been. I explained that I did not know the area of the married quarters and he told me where to go: 'Straight up the main road, second left, third right etc.' … that's where it all went wrong! I lost the way and marched the entire company down a cul-de-sac! It was a long road and I did not realise that it was a cul-de-sac until the end.

But I had successfully counter-marched the band; they were in between the first platoon and all would have been well if the RSM had left it to me, but he ran up, shouting 'Corporal, Corporal! Stop the band! Stop the band!' At the time, I only had about ten days left to do, but the way the RSM went at me, I thought I would be in the glasshouse for weeks. Not funny then, but funny now!

Harold points out that many of the funny incidents in TV programmes like *The Army Game*, that may have seemed incredible to the outsider, were true or, at least, believable. This series struck the right note with the men who had done National Service and their families, who had heard some of the stories. It was created by Sid Colin who had served in the RAF during the Second World War and ran from 1957–1961. *The Army Game* was based around a social cross section of army conscripts in Hut 29 of the Surplus Ordnance Depot at Nether Hopping. The group included Pte 'Cupcake' Cook (Norman Rossington), Pte 'Popeye' Popplewell (Bernard Bresslaw), Pte 'Excused Boots' Bisley (Alfie Bass), Pte Hatchett (Charles Hawtrey) and William Hartnell as Sgt Major Bullimore.

*Carry On Sergeant*, released in 1958, was a cinema spin-off from *The Army Game* and the first Carry On film. Kenneth Williams, Charles Hawtrey, Hattie Jacques, Kenneth Connor and Terry Scott, who were in this film, went on to be part of the regular Carry On team. Norman Rossington and William Hartnell, who appeared in *Carry On Sergeant* as Sergeant Major Grimshaw, did not continue with the Carry On series.

Joan Munro recalls the impression made on a proud little girl by her soldier brother:

I remember my oldest brother coming home on leave from his time in National Service in the Royal Signals. He was my hero, especially when I saw him in his dress uniform when we went to meet him when he came home on leave to Lime Street station.

# 18

# BEING A TEENAGER: MUSIC, DANCING AND YOUTH CLUBS

The late fifties was the period in which teenagers really began to be seen as a separate group from children or adults. This was, in part, the result of the high birth rate after the Second World War; this baby boom generation were entering their teenage years towards the end of the 1950s. They were seen as a target audience by the entertainment business, especially the music scene.

Towards the end of the 1950s, special music programmes for teenagers began to be broadcast on television. *The Six-Five Special* was a first attempt by the BBC to produce a programme with rock 'n' roll music aimed at teenagers. It was put out on Saturday evening at 6.05 p.m. and was introduced by Pete Murray with: 'Time to jive on the old Six-Five!'

The introduction showed a steam train accompanied by rock 'n' roll music with the lyrics:

'The Six-Five Special's comin' down the line
The Six-Five Special's right on time...'

Lonnie Donegan, Marty Wilde and Tommy Steele were among those who appeared on *The Six-Five Special*.

The producer, Jack Good, resigned in 1958 and went to ITV to create *Oh Boy!* The BBC had insisted on the inclusion of some information and educational material on *The Six Five Special*. Now Jack Good was able to produce a programme with non-stop music, which rapidly became much more popular with teenagers.

As well as Lonnie Donegan, Cliff Richard, Brenda Lee, Billy Fury, The Drifters (who later became The Shadows) and the Vernons Girls all appeared on *Oh Boy!*

The Vernons Girls was a choir of about sixteen girls, formed in Liverpool at Vernons Football Pools Company, and were both popular and successful. They released an LP in 1958 on Parlophone which included standards like We'll Gather Lilacs. They also acted as backing singers for several artistes. Later, the group reduced in number, reformed under various names, and moved into more modern music, but there must be a number of women today who had a brief experience of show business as the original Vernons Girls.

*Juke Box Jury* began on BBC in 1959. It was a programme with a celebrity panel of four people, who pronounced their opinion as to whether recently released records would be a hit or a miss. Its signature tune was Hit and Miss by the John Barry Seven Plus Four. The programme was chaired by David Jacobs, a disc jockey, who was thirty-three in 1959. One of the regular panellists, Susan Stranks, was twenty-one in 1959 and she had been included to 'give a teenager's view'. Although it was watched because there were so few 'pop' programmes at the time, *Juke Box Jury* lacked the excitement of *The Six-Five Special* and *Oh Boy!* To some extent, teenagers resented the attempt to influence their judgement and record-buying choices.

Enid Johnston remembers:

Coffee bars started to appear and my friends and I used to go to two in Garston – the Idle Hour in Seddon Road and the Rendezvous in Woolton Road, where we would meet friends for a coffee or, maybe, a milkshake. Many churches held their own dances on Saturday nights and two of our favourites were St Barnabas on Penny Lane and Holy Trinity in Church Road. Occasionally, Garston Swimming Baths would cover the big pool and dances would be held there. We particularly enjoyed the New Year's Eve dances. We used to go to Traditional Jazz at Picton Hall on Sunday evenings, having been to church or Bible class earlier in the day, to hear the popular jazz bands of the day – the Merseysippi Jazz Band or Mick Mulligan and his Magnolia Jazz Band.

Agnes Jones remembers more trusting times:

We went dancing but only to the Locarno, the Rialto and Reece's. The Grafton was the haunt of Teddy boys so 'nice' people didn't go there! We'd meet strange boys at the dance and let them take us home. It's a wonder we didn't end up murdered on the bomb sites. But we always felt safe then.

Derek Jeffery lived with his parents, Muriel and Albert, in Portrush Road, Tuebrook. He remembers the radio as a source of music:

There were many vocalists – David Whitfield, Guy Mitchell, Ronnie Hilton, bands like that of Edmundo Ros, and songs like Mocking Bird Hill; Rose, Rose, I Love You; Cool Water; and She Wears Red Feathers! My mother enjoyed the music of the theatre organ, featured regularly on the radio with Reginald Dixon and Stanley Tudor.

Margaret Dunford remembers: 'We got a radiogram in the fifties. We only had two records at first. One was Diana by Paul Anka and the other was Little Darlin' by The Diamonds.'

Pauline Bennett recalls music at home: 'I remember our big gramophone and, when I was young, thought that the artiste had to sing the song personally when you put on the record.'

When she was older, entertainment also happened outside the home: 'In the late 1950s, we went to Billy Martin's Dance School, usually on a Friday night – homework could wait – we had a fantastic time!'

Billy Martin's Dance School in Derby Lane was just one of the popular places where people could learn to dance. Constance Millington's dance school in Merton Road, Bootle was equally well patronised.

June Buckley remembers her eldest sister:

Olive used to do the jive in the back garden with my cousin and she used to wear really 'sticky-out' skirts with loads of net underskirts and we used to listen to records; I can remember lots of Elvis records being played.

John Halley remembers the local youth club:

We met in the council hall in the grounds of St Oswald's Church in Netherton. We had an old radiogram playing records. I remember learning to jive, jeans, suede shoes, Buddy Holly glasses and Tony Curtis hairstyles. At half-time there were refreshments. No alcoholic drinks, just a bottle of Vimto, sandwiches and cake.

Hazel Rimmer went to County Road Methodist Church:

The youth club was very popular; there was dancing, [it is] where I learnt to dance. Usually, once a month we had a speaker; some of the popular footballers of the day from Liverpool and Everton came along, much to the delight of the boys. I met my husband at the youth club. Dances and concerts were also held on a Saturday evening for families and friends.

Bobbie Binks had a special link with the Fazakerley Cottage Homes: 'My father had been an inmate of the Cottage Homes; he was one of five in his family who were moved from the Walton Workhouse.'

In the 1880s, the Fazakerley Cottage Homes had been opened to provide for children who were in the workhouse because of the poverty, illness or death of their parents. At this time, plans were also made for the building of Olive Mount Children's Home. In 1937, both were placed under the jurisdiction of the Liverpool Education Committee.

Bobbie remembers the Cottage Homes Youth Club, which was open to local young people:

It was a fabulous place to meet girls, listen to music, play snooker, darts or table tennis. They had a big swimming pool that we could use whenever we liked and I played for the Cottage Homes Football Team. The manager, Mr Greatorex, was well known at that time, and violence and everything associated with it was unknown.

Ken Greatorex was, for many years, the Deputy Superintendent of the Cottage Homes and also the goalie for Wrexham Football Club. He is remembered with respect and affection by many of the children who grew up in the Homes and as someone who was always ready to praise effort and achievement.

Anne McCormick remembers a lively social scene for young teenagers:

We used to go to youth clubs in Speke. My sister went to a church club, while I went to one which was held in the school. I loved dancing from an early age. In school we did country dancing, but as the American type rock 'n' roll came into popularity, with the Everly Brothers, Elvis and others, I used to jive at about twelve or thirteen, in the youth club. I also recall going to the Locarno on a Sunday afternoon and dancing to Bobby Vee and Del Shannon. I was only about thirteen, so was not allowed out to night-time events, so this fitted the bill as far as I was concerned. I did, however, go to the Orrell Park Ballroom one night, when I was about thirteen, with my cousin from Walton. When I was older, it was Hollyoak Hall on Smithdown Road, where all the Liverpool groups would play.

Pat Williams has vivid memories of being a teenager:

There were plenty of youth clubs and local dances and the lads would all line up along one wall and the girls along another. The lad would always ask the girl to dance and if you didn't like the look of him he would face the very public humiliation of you saying no. There was no alcohol at these events. I can't remember ever seeing people sneak drink in. We had a local dance near where we lived and we are privileged to have watched famous names like The Beatles, Billy Fury, Gerry and the Pacemakers and Rory Storm and the Hurricanes – all for sixpence.

Music was a big part of our lives. You could go to the record shop and stand in one of the booths and listen to the record before you purchased it; most of us didn't have the money to buy but we listened anyway. I had two records; one was Elvis Presley and the other, Tommy Steele.

We wore full skirts, pretty blouses and feminine clothes. I made a lot of my own things as we were all taught to sew from an early age and material was cheap. We had huge lace petticoats and they were trimmed with tulle. We starched the tulle or soaked it in sugar and water to make it stiff so that it would stick out.

We had to be in early, usually about 10-11 p.m. My dad used to stand on the step waiting for me and I hated it if, when I turned the corner, he would be there.

Despite all these restrictions, most of us were happy. I started nursing at eighteen and I had to live in the Nurses' Home. We had to sign a book before we went out and we had to be in at 10 p.m.

Philip Baker remembers the musical consequences of a holiday in Italy:

In 1958, I managed to save enough to buy a one-way rail ticket to the French Riviera. Two days at the cheapest pension in Cannes was enough to convince me that my money would run out very quickly.

Fortunately, on the second day, I met an Italian of my own age, who was hitch-hiking to Italy to visit relatives. He told me that prices in Italy were half those in France and proposed that I should accompany him hitchhiking to Italy. As we approached the first large town on the Italian side of the border – San Remo – I decided to go no further.

The annual San Remo song contest had finished the week before, so I had no difficulty in finding a cheap place to stay. I spent an enjoyable week there during which every jukebox in the town seemed to be continually playing the song that had just won the annual contest, known there as Nel blu dipinto di blu.

When the next payday came around, I decided I would like to buy the record I had heard so often in San Remo but, since the song was completely unknown in Britain at that time, it wasn't clear how I could do that. I visited the record shop nearest to where I worked – NEMS at the junction of Mathew Street and Whitechapel. The assistant I spoke to said he would have to call his boss, who turned out to be a softly spoken man, aged between twenty-five and thirty, whose speech had not the slightest trace of a Liverpool accent. He seemed extraordinarily pleased that someone had come into his shop to ask for something unusual. He searched various trade publications and discovered that the record was to be released in Britain on an obscure label (Durium) a few days later. He said he would order it for me, and that I should telephone in about ten days' time to enquire whether it had arrived. 'What name should I ask for?' – Brian Epstein was his reply. The name meant nothing to me at the time but, four or five years later, it was in the popular press constantly as the name of The Beatles' manager. The record duly arrived. A couple of months later this song was a major hit in Britain but under the title Volare.

In the second half of the 1950s, a major feature of life in Liverpool was coffee bars. The most interesting of these was called the Basement, not far from Skelhorne Street Bus Depot. Other clubs we visited included the Jacaranda, which featured a live steel band, and the Beacon, a place frequented by black US soldiers, many of whom brought musical instruments with them and collectively entertained us with jazz. It was the nearest thing to New Orleans that Liverpool could offer.

Skiffle was becoming popular at this time and I, like many others, acquired a guitar and joined a group, doubling on washboard. The band was called The Caldonies, the name coming from the brand name of the guitar owned by the leader of the group. The Cavern started to have skiffle nights once a week. Five or six groups would be invited to play for up to half an hour each. They were not paid but, at the end of the evening the owner of the club would give a small cash prize to the group he judged the best. The Caldonies won the prize on two or three occasions. Musically we were as bad as any other skiffle group but, unlike them, we had made skiffle versions of some old songs from the American South and included these in our repertoire, which is probably what the Cavern owner liked. No scouts from record companies ever signed us up but two of the songs we did were to enjoy major commercial success a few years later – Cottonfields and House of the Rising Sun – but we didn't have anything to do with that.

Peter McGuiness, fifteen in 1950, remembers jazz music and the days before the Cavern became world-renowned:

A couple of my friends were jazz fans and, although I was far from an enthusiast, I did accompany them to a few concerts. I heard Ken Colyer at The Pavilion, the Merseysippi Jazz Band at the Temple Bar in Dale Street, and I went with them on two occasions to the Cavern. On the first occasion, I heard Kenny Baker, the famous British trumpeter. We sat on chairs in rows. The audience was very serious, mostly male and with quite a wide age range present; certainly not all teenagers. When I went to the Cavern for the second time, I heard the legendary American blues singer, Big Bill Broonzy. This time the audience stood and there were more girls, but still a wide age range.

I never went to the Cavern again and never heard the famous Liverpool Sound. However, I can boast that I have been to the Cavern, although the music, audience and atmosphere were very different from the 1960s when it became famous throughout the world.

Robin Bird lived in New Brighton, but continued to attend school in Liverpool. He remembers 'bunking off' in his lunchtime to go to the Cavern Club: 'With hindsight, the best thing I ever did – seeing The Beatles, Gerry and the Pacemakers, the Big Three, Faron's Flamingos and the like!'

Liverpool's children of the 1950s were growing up and stood poised on the threshold of the 1960s, when their vibrant and very special city would become the centre of the universe and they would become the envy of all young people worldwide!

# BIBLIOGRAPHY

Bailey, F.A., & Millington, R., *The Story of Liverpool* (The Merseyside Press, 1957)

Bastable, J., (ed) *Yesterday's Britain* (The Reader's Digest Association, 1998)

Good Housekeeping, *The Best of the 1950s* (Collins & Brown, 2008)

Opie, R., *The 1950s Scrapbook* (PI Global Publishing, 1998)

Pressley, A., *The 50s and 60s: The Best of Times* (Michael O'Mara Books, 1999)

Russell, P., 'Liverpool's Past: A Magical History Tour' in Grant, A. & Grey, C. (eds), *The Mersey Sound* (Open House Press, 2007)

Russell, P., *Liverpool's Children in the Second World War* (The History Press, 2009)